THE NATURE OF ANGELS

THE
NATURE OF ANGELS

EIGHT ADDRESSES

BY

ALEXANDER WHYTE, LL.D.

 Baker Books

A Division of Baker Book House Co
Grand Rapids, Michigan 49516

Reprinted 1976, 1995 by Baker Books
a division of Baker Book House Company
P.O. Box 6287, Grand Rapids, MI 49516-6287

Printed in the United States of America

ISBN 0-8010-5107-X

Cover artwork:

The Annunciation (detail) by Giannicola di Paolo (Umbrian, c. 1460–1544)
1510/1515, oil on panel, National Gallery of Art, Washington. Samuel H.
Kress Collection. Used with permission.

FOREWORD

Of late I have had time to go over some of my husband's unpublished papers and, encouraged by the opinion of friends, both of those whose allegiance is to the old order of things, and of those with young, modern, scientific minds, I have come to the conclusion that some of them merit publication.

The modern world has to some extent created for itself a bogey of Victorian religion, compacted, it would seem, in equal parts of pharisaism, emotionalism, and insincerity.

To fresh, young, vigorous minds seeking only for truth and reality, I venture in this small volume to offer for their consideration a sample of the spiritual food which nourished hundreds of young men and women in Scotland in the last thirty years of the nineteenth century.

From a large mass of possible material I have chosen mainly that which, from various angles, deals with the relation of the human spirit to those great hierarchies which domi-

nate the unseen world, and which have ever
mediated its power and blessing, from the
day when Jacob, sleeping on the pillow of
stone, saw the angels of God ascending and
descending upon a ladder which reached from
earth to heaven, until Francis Thompson saw
the same " traffic "

'Twixt heaven and Charing Cross.

The first address on " The Use of the
Imagination in Religion " is of the nature of
an introduction to the whole subject. " The
Good Angel (or Dæmon) of Socrates " en-
deavours to assimilate the interior Voice
which directed Socrates with what is called
our conscience. The group on the Nature of
Angels—part of a long series on the Epistle
to the Hebrews—" Gabriel comes to Mary
and Joseph," and " The Angel of the Agony "
move within the circle of the Old and New
Testament experience. " Fulness of Joy " I
have included simply because I like it.

A Bibliography is added for those who
would carry their study of angels into wider
fields. The subject is so vast and so compelling that no one should take it up who is
unwilling to have his or her whole life dominated by it.

All religions have taken cognizance of these great sources of power. Indeed, under one form or another they have presided at the birth of all religions with any claim to universality.

Of the effect of vision on intellectual outlook and upon character there is no more startling fact recorded than that in the life of St Thomas Aquinas.

Some time before his death, as Aquinas was celebrating Mass in Naples, he had a wonderful spiritual experience. The nature of it is not detailed, but the result of it was that he put his inkhorn and writing materials upon a shelf and never wrote or dictated another word of the *Summa*.

My writing days are over, for such things have been revealed to me that all I have written and taught seems but of small account to me, wherefore I hope in my God that even as the end has come to my teaching so it may soon come to my life.

The *Summa* breaks off in the middle of the Sacrament of Penitence, and therefore leaves out the Sacraments of Extreme Unction, Ordination and Matrimony, and the Doctrine of the Final State.[1]

[1] *Dante and Aquinas*. P. H. Wicksteed, Jowett Lectures, 1911.

This volume is merely a sign-post. It makes no attempt to grapple with the deep questions of being—which when unravelled will one day throw light on problems of human personality. Any easy explanation, such as is given by some that angels are all human beings in another form, is ruled out by the writer of the Epistle to the Hebrews, where it is said, " He took not on him the nature of angels," and his (or is it her) principle that they do not rule as man was meant to rule the material world. Their sphere is elsewhere. Which things the angels desire to look into.

The religions of Judah and of Islam are full of angel presences. In Iona there is a tradition that Columba received instruction from the Angel of the Pole Star on *Sithean Mor*, and Joan of Arc's life was dominated throughout by her voices and visions. Here is Bernard Shaw's explanation :

Robert de Baudricourt. What did you mean when you said that St Catherine and St Margaret talked to you every day ?

Joan. They do.

Robert. What are they like ?

Joan (suddenly obstinate). I will tell you nothing about that : they have not given me leave.

Robert. But you actually see them ; and they talk to you just as I am talking to you ?

Joan. No ; it is quite different. I cannot tell you : you must not ask me about my voices.

Robert. How do you mean ? Voices ?

Joan. I hear voices telling me what to do. They come from God.

Robert. They come from your imagination.

Joan. Of course. That is how the messages of God come to us.

Poulengey. Checkmate.[1]

From cover to cover the Bible is full of the " many splendoured " orders of the angels, from the tragic day when :

The Lord God drove out the man ; and he placed at the east of the garden of Eden Cherubim and a flaming sword which turned every way, to keep the way of the Tree of Life,

until when the final revelation is complete, and John has seen the Holy City descending out of heaven from God, it has at its gates twelve angels, and he ends :

When I had heard and seen I fell down to worship before the feet of the angel which showed me these things. Then said he unto me, " See thou do it not, for I am thy fellow servant and of thy brethren the prophets and of them which keep the sayings of this book : Worship God."

The whole undivided Church of Christ sings daily in her Communion Service :

[1] *St Joan*, Bernard Shaw, Scene i.

Therefore with Angels and Archangels and with all the company of heaven, we laud and magnify thy glorious Name, evermore praising thee and saying :

"Holy, holy, holy, Lord God of Hosts, heaven and earth are full of Thy glory."

We cannot here do more than allude to the place which these spiritual powers hold in the East, whether as Devas or as Boddhisattvas, or in the oracles of Egypt and of Greece.

A visit to the British Museum will greatly repay, especially by the study of the magnificent Chinese fresco of the three attendant Boddhisattvas who watch the coming of Buddha.

It is a large part of the pain and loss of modern life that, burrowing too much in the dirt-heaps of Mammon, or burying itself in pigeon-holed academic knowledge, or trying to discover the meaning of life in the Freudian underground channels, the human consciousness has lost its own true ancient power to see the wings which flash through the ether, or to catch the harmonies of the music of the spheres.

But this condition cannot be for long.

Where there is no vision the people perish.

Surely it was of the soul of man that Francis Thompson sang :

> O Lily of the King, low lies thy silver wing
> And long hath been the night of thy undoing,

and it is to the soul of man that Keats' ode is dedicate :

> O latest born and loveliest far
> Of all Olympus' faded hierarchy.

Psyche awaits her great lover, and the ministry of angels is now at work clearing away the cobwebs that veil her vision, and, as scavengers, to " sweep the Bridegroom's path."

" I am confident that, by what has been said, I shall strike the sparks of the Divine Fire stored up in Thee."

J. E. W.

CONTENTS

I

THE USE OF THE IMAGINATION IN RELIGION

> Die Geisterwelt ist nicht verschlossen !
> Dein Sinn ist Zu, dein Herz ist todt !
> Auf ! bade, Schuler, unverdrossen
> Die irdische Brust im Morgenroth !
>
> GOETHE's *Faust*.

I assert, for myself, that I do not behold the outward creation, and that to me it is hindrance and not action. "What ! " it will be questioned, " when the sun rises, do you not see a round disc of fire somewhat like a guinea ? " Oh ! no, no ! I see an innumerable company of the heavenly host crying, " Holy, holy, holy is the Lord God Almighty ! " I question not my corporeal eye any more than I would question a window concerning a sight. I look through it, and not with it.—BLAKE, *A Vision of the Last Judgment.*

THE USE OF THE IMAGINATION IN RELIGION

" The evidence of things not seen."—HEB. xi. 1.

[This address was given to students in New Greyfriars' Church, Edinburgh, 1st February 1903.]

" THE Use of the Imagination in Religion " is the subject of my discourse. But, before I enter upon that—let me glance, for a moment, at the use of the imagination in science and in literature. I shall not presume to speak in my own name on matters of science. But I will quote the testimonies and the acknowledgments of two eminent men of science, who are, at the same time, the masters of a clear and an eloquent English style. Sir Benjamin Brodie, in his Presidential Address to the Royal Society, has this remarkable passage : " Physical investigation, more than anything else, helps to teach us the actual value and the right use of the imagination : that wondrous faculty, which, when it is properly controlled by experience and reflection, becomes the noblest attribute of

man. Imagination is the source of all poetic
genius, and it has been the instrument of
many of our most remarkable discoveries in
science. Without the aid of imagination
Isaac Newton would never have invented
fluxions : nor Humphry Davy have decom-
posed the earths and the alkalies. Nor
would Christopher Columbus have ever found
another Continent." And Professor Tyndale,
in his eloquent discourse before the British
Association, has this equally apposite passage :
" Bounded and conditioned by co-operant
reason, imagination becomes the mightiest
instrument of the physical discoverer. Newton's passage from a falling apple to a
falling moon was, at the outset, a leap of the
imagination. When Sir William Thomson [1]
tries to place the ultimate particles of matter
between his compass-points, and to apply to
them a scale of millimetres, he is powerfully
aided by his imagination. And in much that
has been said of recent years about proto-
plasm, and life, we have the outgoings of the
imagination guided and controlled by the
known analogies of science."

Some years ago I was climbing a high,

[1] Lord Kelvin.

hollowed-out hill near Ballachulish, along
with my friend Mr Peyton of Broughty
Ferry. The great scooped-out hillside looked
to my uninstructed and unimaginative eye
like an unaccountable freak of nature in
ancient rock. But, when my gifted companion cast a geologist's eye on the gigantic
egg-shell, he saw the great glacial-plough of
the Ice Age tearing out the soft inside of that
great hill and leaving the hard outside to
tell its eloquent story to him who had the
eye to read its rocky record. That great
scooped-out shell of hard rock was to my
talented friend the evidence of things no
longer seen ; no longer seen—but to the eye
of the scientific imagination.

It is the same in the world of literature.
Our every word—without which we can
neither think nor speak nor write nor read
—are all themselves, originally, the product
of the imagination. It was a fruitful ob-
servation of Coleridge, who was a man of
unequalled philosophical and literary imagination himself, that a certain " visual image,"
as he called it, lies buried at the root of every
single word we speak and write. And he
urged on his generation that an instructed

and an imaginative glance at that buried and forgotten image is absolutely indispensable to him who would either think or write or read aright. And Archbishop Trench, taking up that philological doctrine from his revered master, published his well-known " Study of Words "—a book, the first reading of which has been an intellectual and a spiritual epoch in the lives of tens of thousands of its delighted readers.

And then, simply to name the greatest works of genius of the ancient and modern world is to point to so many triumphs of the literary imagination. Wordsworth has said somewhere—I think in one of his famous Prefaces—that Homer is the father of poetry because he always sings " with his eye on the object." That is to say, Homer always sees, and that with an intensely imaginative eye, what he forthwith sings to us. And thus it is that Homer sings to us as no other singer has ever sung—unless it is Dante. And, if Dante is more to us than Homer, it is because his superb imagination was first sanctified and was then directed, not upon " things seen and temporal, but upon things unseen and eternal."

And then our common Christian people
have, in their own tongue in which they were
born, those two great triumphs of an evangelical imagination, *The Pilgrim's Progress*
and *The Holy War* : two books of evangelical
genius that will stand to all time among the
masterpieces of literature. That the life of
faith on this earth is like a pilgrimage, and
that all true believers are so many " strangers
and sojourners " with God on the earth—
that expressive figure of speech fills Holy
Scripture and all religious literature, from
Abraham's day down to our own day. But
one man only has had the genius experi-
mentally and imaginatively and realisingly
to see so as to describe the whole of that
pilgrimage, and that man was John Bunyan.
Also, that the life of true godliness is a
constant warfare and battle, the Prophets
and the Psalms and the Gospels and the
Epistles and all the diaries and devotions of
all God's saints, unite to tell us. But the
author of *The Holy War* alone has seen
and shared in that war, so as to tell us
what he saw and suffered, till that truly great
book stands beside *The Pilgrim's Progress*, a
masterpiece of spiritual imagination and a

classic of the purest and most powerful
English style :

> For my part, I myself was in the town,
> Both when 'twas set up, and when pulling down.
> .   .   .   .   what is here in view,
> Of mine own knowledge, I dare say is true.
>   I saw the Prince's armed men come down
> By troops, by thousands, to besiege the town ;
> I saw the captains, heard the trumpets sound,
> And how his forces covered all the ground.
> Yea, how they set themselves in battle-'ray,
> I shall remember to my dying day.
> I saw who wounded were, and who were slain ;
> And who, when dead, would come to life again.
> Tell you of all, I neither will, nor can I.
> But by what here I say, you well may see,
> That Mansoul's matchless wars no fables be.

And then, when we come to the highest
literature of all, we find the imaginations of
holy men of old taken up into the hand of
the Holy Ghost and made a vehicle of divine
revelation and a means of transmitting that
revelation to the minds and the hearts of
men. To begin at the beginning : " By faith
which is the evidence of things not seen we
understand that the worlds were framed by the
word of God, so that things which are seen
were not made of things which do appear."
" Gird up now thy loins like a man ; for I
will demand of thee, and answer thou me.

Where wast thou when I laid the foundations of the earth ? Declare, if thou hast understanding. Who hath laid the measures thereof, if thou knowest ? Or who hath stretched the line upon it ? Whereupon are the foundations thereof fastened ? Or who laid the corner stone thereof : when the morning stars sang together and all the sons of God shouted for joy " ?

It was our own honoured and beloved Hugh Miller's instructed and devout and brilliant imagination that first gave us the true key in Scotland to open up the hid treasures of truth and of beauty that lay locked up in the imaginative prologue to the Book of Genesis. Till we are now able to take up the words of Wisdom herself into a sanctified and soaring imagination and say, " When He prepared the heavens, I was there : when He set a compass upon the face of the depth : when He gave to the sea His decree : when He appointed the foundations of the earth. Then I was by Him, as one brought up with Him, rejoicing always before Him : rejoicing in the habitable part of His earth : and my delights were with the sons of men."

And, as " all that is within us," as all

man's mind and heart was made instrumental in the production of Holy Scripture—from Moses to John—so did imagination get her own high place from one stage of revelation to another, and from one outpouring of inspiration to another. And just as scientifically instructed men can see the past of this earth with their scientifically anointed eyes, and just as men of literature can look back ages and recognise the splendid service that imagination has performed in their world of things, so the instructed and open-eyed and imaginative student of Holy Scripture can see his favourite faculty at constant work in the revealing hand of the Spirit of grace and truth. All down the books of Holy Scripture such a student delights to see the use to which the imagination was put, and the indispensable work that it did and that it alone would have been able to do. There are whole books of the Bible of a sanctified and inspired imagination " all compact "—for example, Job, Isaiah, Ezekiel. Without the imagination at its very highest sanctification and service-ableness, we would never have had those wonderful books.

And not to dwell on our Lord's parables, nor on Paul's Epistles, all gleaming as they are with his sanctified genius, we come to the Book of Revelation. A book in which the heaven-illuminated imagination of that aged seer lays this shining copestone on the glorious edifice of Holy Scripture: " Open thou mine eyes, that I may behold wondrous things out of thy law ! "

And then, what a fundamental, and what an all-essential part does this wonderful faculty perform in all true prayer and praise. And what an incomparable and inexhaustible scope do prayer and praise and all manner of communion with God offer and afford to this most shining and soaring of all the faculties of the sanctified soul ! The truth is, without the constant and increasing use of this supreme talent of the sanctified soul, no true prayer can be offered and no true praise can be paid. It is true we may be employing this great talent and faculty of our minds when we are not reflecting on its use : we may employ it even before we know that we possess it. But we would perform all our devotions far more intelligently and far more fruitfully if we studied all the capacities and

all the possibilities of our minds and called on
" all that is within us," as David did, to
praise and magnify the Lord.

Listen to what a great master in Israel has
said to us on this matter. " Seeing our
imaginations have great power over our
hearts, and can mightily affect us with their
representations, it would be of great use to
you if, at the beginning of your devotions,
you were to imagine to yourself some such
representations as might heat and warm your
heart. As thus : Be still, and imagine to
yourself that you see the heavens open and
the glorious thorns of Seraphim and Cherubim
before the throne of God. Help your imagination with such passages of Scripture as
these also :—I beheld, and lo, a great multitude which no man could number stood
before the throne and before the Lamb,
clothed with white robes, and palms in their
hands ; and cried with a loud voice, saying,
Salvation to our God which sitteth upon
the throne and unto the Lamb. Think
upon all this : see all this, till your imagination has carried you above the clouds and
has placed you up in your own place—among
those heavenly beings, and has made you to

long to take part in their heavenly music. Always begin your psalm with these imaginations, and at every verse of it imagine yourself amongst those heavenly companions, and that you with your poor, low voice are singing with such splendour on earth what they are singing in heaven.

"Again, sometimes imagine that you had been one of those who joined with our Blessed Saviour when He ' sang an hymn.' Strive to imagine to yourself with what majesty He looked : and fancy that you had stood beside Him and had seen His face and heard His voice.

"And yet again, sometimes imagine yourself that you see David with his hands on his harp and his eyes fixed upon heaven, calling in transport upon all creation, sun and moon, light and darkness, day and night, men and angels, to join with his enraptured soul in praising the Lord of Heaven."

Thus far—as all his enriched readers will recognise—a very prince of devotional writers.[1] And I will only add to that such an expansion and application of his principle as this :—

Let us carry into all our prayers and

[1] William Law.

praises that visualising and realising practice
that Coleridge has taught us. Let us be
philologically and philosophically, as well as
devotionally, honest and true with ourselves
and with the God of truth. Let us seek for,
till we see, the " visual image " that lies at
the root of all God's names and attributes
and words and works. And at the root of
all our own words, back again toward God.
Let us see what we say and then say what
we see. Let our inward eye affect our inward heart. When we say " O God ! " let
us see Him on whom we so call. When we
say " for Christ's Sake," let our eyes flash
faster than lightning to where He once hung
on the tree : and then, to where He now sits
on the throne. When we say that " our sins
are ever before us," let them be before us.
When we say " pardon mine iniquity, for
it is very great," let our broken hearts lie
in the dust under the great aggravation of
our sins. When we say " heaven," let us
that instant look up. When we say " hell,"
let us that instant look down. Never wash
your hands without saying, " I shall be
clean." Never see snow without saying,
" I shall be one day whiter than that spot-

less snow." Nor the sun rise without saying,
" When I awake, I shall be satisfied with
His likeness." " Behold! Thou desirest
truth in the inward parts: and in the hidden
part Thou shalt make me to know wisdom."

And, then, once you really begin to employ
and exercise your emancipated and ennobled
imagination and your holy heart upon
Almighty God in that way, you will never
be able to lift either your imagination or
your heart off Him. You will say to yourself continually and to all that is within you,
" to Whom shall we go ? " You will find
yourself saying continually, " Thou hast
made us for Thyself, and now we have found
all our rest and peace and consolation and
satisfaction in Thee." Yes: and you will
come to these other magnificent words of
Saint Augustine :—*Deus ubique est : et totus
ubique est.* God is everywhere, and He is
wholly everywhere. And then, God's presence ever with you : and His whole presence
ever with you will take possession of both
your imagination and your heart, till sometimes, whether you are in the body or out of
the body—you cannot tell : you are now so
immersed in God and He is so immersed in you.

Men and brethren! If Almighty God is
everywhere and if He is wholly everywhere
—what a vision! What an imagination!
What an ocean of truth and love and blessedness is that! Our God and our Father: the
Fountain of our life: and the Source and
Well-spring of all our blessedness. "Who is
a God like unto Thee!" And what manner
of men ought we to be!

O! my brethren! Since these things are
so. Let us know ourselves! Let us put our
true and proper value upon ourselves! Let
us continually tell ourselves, in Whose Image
we were made, and to what an end and intention of His, He made us. Let us measure
from what we have fallen. And let us feast
our mind and heart on that to which we are
redeemed and restored.

And among a multitude of other great
and precious talents and endowments, let us
ponder well the supreme and soaring endow-
ment of the imagination. For, it is nothing
less than a human image of the Divine Omni-
science. It answers to the all-seeing Eye of
the Almighty God Himself: and His all-
seeing Eye answers and responds to it. And
then, think of this, I beseech you. This—

that you have your imagination in your own hand. It is in your own hand and power and choice to open and turn your inward eye as it pleases you. You can debauch and pollute your imagination till both your heart and your life are filled full with all the corruption and uncleanness of the second death. Or you can fill your imagination with visions of beauty—created and uncreated—visions of love and holiness and heaven—till you are rewarded, at last, with the Beatific Vision itself. " While we look not at the things which are seen, but at the things which are not seen : for the things which are seen are temporal, but the things which are not seen are eternal."

II

THE GOOD ANGEL (DÆMON) OF SOCRATES

" The Spirit of Man is the candle of the Lord."—
PROVERBS.

THE GOOD ANGEL (DÆMON) OF SOCRATES

[*First given to the St George's Literary Society on 4th November 1886, and fifteen times afterwards in various places, including Mansfield College, Oxford, on 1st March 1891.*]

I

XENOPHON and Plato are our best authorities for the life of Socrates. Strange to say, Thucydides, though a contemporary of Socrates, never once mentions his name. And though Aristophanes repeatedly introduces Socrates into his comedies, yet the representation there given of the great philosopher by the great buffoon is worse than valueless, for it is both unjust and untrue. Plutarch and Diogenes are late, legendary and uncritical; and often as Socrates is referred to in the Greek and Roman classics, and in the Christian Fathers, they really add nothing to what Xenophon and Plato have told us of their famous master.

Xenophon, "the military brother of the Socratic family," was both a soldier and an author, and he did noble service to his

country in both capacities. He had left us
The Cyropædia, The Œconomicus, and *The
Memorabilia*; and, though the composition
of these works does not place Xenophon in
the very first rank of classical authors, yet
the value of these treatises to the student of
Greek history, Greek life, and Greek manners
cannot be overestimated. All our schoolboys know Xenophon's *Cyropædia*; it were
well that all their sisters read and pondered
his *Œconomicus*; and as for his *Memorabilia*,
all our philosophers have it by heart. The
four books of the *Memorabilia* are a quite
priceless possession to the admirer of Socrates.
Boswell's *Life of Dr Johnson* is perhaps the
English book that most resembles Xenophon's
Memorabilia of Socrates. There is in the
Greek book the same profound reverence of
the scholar for the master that we have in
the English book; the same affectionate
assiduity and fidelity in recording the utterances of the master; the same chivalry in
his defence; and something of the same
success in painting an artless but incomparable portrait of a great man. There is a
story told by Strabo—though I am sorry to
see that Grote discredits it—a story to the

effect that when the Greek army, in which both Socrates and Xenophon were serving, was defeated at Delium, and Xenophon was in danger of being taken prisoner, Socrates took the wounded lad on his broad shoulders and bore him to a place of safety. If that was so, Xenophon has nobly repaid the debt; for in the pages of his able and affectionate book he has vindicated the good name and extended the fame of his honoured master to all future ages. "Xenophon, the son of Gryllus," says Diogenes Lærtius in his *Lives of the Philosophers*, "was a citizen of Athens, and of the deme of Erchia; he was a man of great modesty, and as handsome as can be imagined. They say that when he was a young man Socrates met him one day in a narrow lane when he put his stick across it to prevent him from passing, and as the philosopher held the youth he asked him if he knew where this and that necessary of life was sold. And, when the youth had answered, Socrates then asked him if he knew where men were made good and virtuous. Confessing he did not know that, Socrates said to him: 'Follow me and learn these things.' And from that time forth

Xenophon became a follower of Socrates."
" And he was the first person," adds Diogenes,
" who took down conversations as they
occurred, and published them, calling them
Memorabilia. He was also the first man
who wrote a history of philosophers."

Of Plato, on the other hand, it may with
simple truth be said that he was too great an
author to be a good authority. Plato was
too great a man himself to be a good biographer of another man, however great. A
far less man than Plato would have made
a far better reporter and biographer of
Socrates. Xenophon was a far less man
than Plato, but it is a question whether his
portrait of Socrates is not truer to the life
than that of Plato.

Plato's writings are the glory of Greek
prose ; and, while Socrates wrote nothing
himself, he is absolutely glorified in every
page that Plato writes ; so glorified indeed,
that we can scarcely distinguish his homely
features in the splendid nimbus that Plato
pours around his head. All the works of
Plato that have come down to us are cast in
the form of dialogues, and in almost every
one of them Socrates is set forth as the

protagonist, the leading debater, the final authority, the master-mind. Suppose that in the plays of Shakespeare, which are the only series of writings we have that can compare with the dialogues of Plato for depth and power and riches and beauty— suppose in them that Hamlet, or some other of Shakespeare's greatest and best creations, had appeared as one of the *dramatis personœ* in all the plays, and that their immortal author had exhausted and surpassed himself in the wealth of intellect and heart he poured out on the world through his favourite and ever-present character—then we would have had in our own literature an analogue to the Socrates of the Platonic Dialogues.

Plato's extant and accepted works consist of some twenty-seven Dialogues ostensibly carried on by Socrates along with or against such men as Plato and Xenophon, Aristophanes and Alcibiades, Protagoras and Prodicus, Apollodorus and Parmenides, along with a host of other men who would have been altogether unknown to us but for the immortality that has been conferred on their names in the titles of some of the Socratic and Platonic Dialogues; such men as

Euthyphro and Ion, Euthydemus and Lysis, Crito and Phædo, Charmides and Phædrus. The splendid series is occupied with such questions as Temperance in the Charmides, Friendship in the Lysis, Virtue in the Meno, Justice in the Republic, Legislation in the Laws, Government in the Politicus, Love in the Phædrus and in the Symposium, Human Nature in the First Alcibiades and Prayer in the Second, Knowledge in the Theaetetus, Duty in the Crito, Holiness in the Euthyphro, and Immortality in the Phædo. And all those subjects are treated by Plato, through Socrates, with a gigantic intellectual strength, and at the same time with a wealth of literary power and resource that makes the writings of Plato a perfect treasure-house of logic and rhetoric, poetry and paradox, humour and pathos, satire and irony, raillery and tenderness, till, as we read and re-read those peerless Dialogues, we come to feel the truth and fitness of the inscription his countrymen put over the grave of Plato, " Here lies a man much too great for envy." And thus it is, as I have already said, that Plato's Dialogues are much too great, much too original, much too rich, much too lofty; in one word, much too Platonic to yield us a good portrait of the man who is so glorified in them. Socrates lives and speaks in every page of Plato, but then, every page of his so shines with intellectual light and moral beauty that we cannot clearly see what is so dazzlingly delivered unto us. Still, Xenophon and Plato are our best authorities for the life of Socrates.

II

The child Socrates was born in a poor man's house in Athens in the year 469 before Christ. Moral Philosophy was born in Greece just about the time that Hebrew Prophecy was expiring in Palestine. Socrates' father, Sophroniscus, was a sculptor, but he must have belonged to the humblest walks of that great Greek art, since his industrious spouse had to eke out her husband's earnings by going out as a midwife. The boy Socrates was early apprenticed to his father's trade; and, if tradition is to be trusted, the youth showed some genius in handling the hammer and the chisel. A beautiful group of draped Graces, that long after stood in the Acropolis,

was popularly believed to have come from
the chisel of Sophroniscus' son.

> Chisel in hand stood a sculptor boy,
> With a marble block before him ;
> And a gleam of joy lit up his eye,
> As an angel dream passed o'er him.
> He carved that dream on the shapeless stone
> With many a sharp incision ;
> That angel dream he had made his own,
> His own that Angel vision.
> Sculptors of Life are we, he said,
> With our souls uncarved before us,
> Waiting the time, till at God's command
> Our life dream passes o'er us.
> If we carve that dream on our shapeless soul,
> With many a sharp incision,
> That angel dream we have made our own,
> Our own that Angel vision.

Even to be born and brought up in the
Athens of that day, though it was only in a
stone-cutter's workshop, was itself a liberal
education ; and we may be sure that young
Socrates neglected nothing that was open to
him of moral and intellectual opportunity.
He seems early to have discovered, to use
his own words, in the lane to Xenophon,
where wisdom and virtue were sold, and he
set himself, with all his might, to possess
himself of those incorruptible treasures.   The
Athenian stone-cutter and his wife had no

such spiritual food to set before their inap-
peasable boy as the call of Samuel or the
dream of Solomon, but what they had they
made diligent use of. The choice of Hercules
would be the entertainment and ensample
of the apprentice artist, and, possessing it,
Socrates was not left without a Divine Witness. " The Light that lighteth every man
that cometh into the world " shone out of
many an ancient page, though, with it all,
young Socrates fell far short of our better
nurtured children with their Bible stories,
their *Pilgrim's Progress*, their *Holy War*,
and their *Paradise Lost and Regained*, on a
Sabbath evening.

Invaluable as the information would be to
us we know next to nothing of the upbringing
and early education of young Socrates, and
all we really know is gathered from occasional
hints and incidental allusions in his recorded
conversations in later life. But there is an
autobiographical fragment in the *Phædo*
which, rightly read, tells volumes as to the
intellectual and religious growth of the young
statuary. " When I was still a youth," he
tells his weeping friends in the prison on the
day of his death, " I had a prodigious desire

to master that department of Philosophy
called Natural Science. This branch of knowledge seemed to me then to have the loftiest
aims ; all its votaries said it was of all
sciences the one that took you closest to the
true causes of things, and laid them bare in
their origin and laws. In those days I was
always agitating myself about the origin of
life, about air and fire and water, about
genera and species, about the brain and
its relations to sight and hearing and smell
and memory and opinion ; till at last I came
to the conclusion that I was utterly and
absolutely unable to get at the bottom of
such things : and besides, in pursuit of them
I was in danger of forgetting the most self-
evident facts.

"About this time I got hold somehow of a
lately published book of Anaxagoras entitled
' First Principles,' or some such promising
name, in which that Philosopher undertook
to explain all about ' The Senses and the
Intellect,' and ' The Emotions and the Will,'
and as I sat down to the book I was delighted above measure at the feast of truth
that I was told was to be set before me :
truth, as I supposed, about myself, ' so fear-

fully and wonderfully made,' and about the
Eternal Mind Who must have made my mind
and me. What hopes, I remember, I set out
with, and how grievously was I disappointed !
For as I proceeded I found my philosophic
master altogether forsaking mind and spirit,
both human and divine, and having recourse
instead to air and ether and water, and other
eccentricities. And, as I read on, I became
more and more confused, till I said to myself that I must take good care else I will
soon become so materialised in my thoughts
as to lose the true eye of my soul altogether.
And, I well remember, that at last I rose up
and said to myself : ' Socrates, thou hadst
better turn thy attention in upon thyself,
and seek in the world of mind the real truth
as to the chief end of thy existence ! ' I am
forced to admit that even the science of mind
is but a looking at truth as ' through a glass
darkly,' but it was the best I could do then,
and I have continued to do it to this day.
My friend Cebes, when I am gone, forget not
my dying words : *Know Thyself*."

Such is Socrates' own account of his con-
version to Moral Philosophy.

The call of Socrates to the philosophic

apostleship is really the commencement of
Socrates' life to us. When the venerable
sage was on his trial he gave his judges an
account of his Divine Call, which in more
ways than one reminds us of the similar
narration that the aged Apostle Paul repeatedly laid before his judges. The Apologies
of Socrates and of Paul differ greatly, but not
more, not so much, as the times and circumstances of the two men differ. Remember
always that you are in Athens in the fifth
century before Christ, and that you are at
the very heart of the dispensation of Pagan-
ism, and you cannot but listen reverently to
Socrates' own account of his Election and Call
to serve God and his generation according
to the will of God. This priceless passage of
Socrates' autobiography comes in best here:

" I dare say, Athenians," he said to the
501 dikasts or jurymen who sat upon his
case, " I dare say that some of you will reply
to me, ' Yes, Socrates, but what is the real
origin of these accusations that are brought
against you ? There must surely have been
something to account for this so serious a
charge. All this talk and all these com-
plaints would never have arisen against you

if you had been like other men : tell us, then, what has been the cause of them, for we should be sorry to judge too hastily of you?' Now, I regard this as a fair challenge, and I will endeavour to explain to you the origin of my name as a philosopher, and of the evil fame that accompanies it. . . . And here, O Men of Athens, I must beg you not to interrupt me, even if I seem to say something that is quite extravagant. For the word which I speak is not mine. I will refer you to a witness who is worthy of credit, and that witness shall be none other than the God of Delphi. You must all have known Chærephon, he was an early friend of mine, and also a friend of yours, for he shared in the exile of the people and returned with you. Well, Chærephon, as you know, was very impetuous in his doings ; and he went to Delphi and boldly asked the Oracle to tell him whether there was anyone wiser than I was, and the Pythian prophetess answered that Socrates was the wisest of men. Chærephon is dead himself, but his brother, who is in court, will confirm the truth of what I am saying. Now, why do I mention this ? Because I am going to explain why I have such an evil name. When I heard the answer, I said to myself, What can the god mean ? and what is the interpretation of his riddle ? For I know that I have no wisdom to be called wisdom, small or great. Then what can he mean when he says that I am the wisest of men ? And yet he is a god, and cannot lie ; that would be against his nature. After long consideration I at last thought of a method of trying the question. I reflected that if I could only find a man wiser than myself, then I might go to the god with a refutation and a discharge in my hand. Then I could say to him, ' Here is a man who is wiser than I am ; but you said that I was the wisest of men.' Accordingly I went to one who had the reputation of wisdom, and observed him—his name I need not mention ; he was a politician whom I selected for examination—and the result was as follows : When I began to talk with him I could not help thinking that he was not really wise, although he was thought wise by many, and wiser still by himself ; and thereupon I tried to explain to him that he thought himself wise, but was really an ignorant and foolish man ; and the consequence was that he hated

me, and his enmity was shared by several of
his party who were present and heard me.
So I left him, saying to myself as I went
away, Well, although I do not suppose that
either of us knows anything aright, yet at
any rate I am better off than he is—for he
knows nothing, and *thinks* he knows, while I
neither *know* nor *think* I know.   Then I
went to another who had still higher philosophical pretensions, and my conclusion was
exactly the same.   I made another enemy of
him, and of all his friends into the bargain.

" Then I went to one man after another,
all the time quite aware of the enmity I was
provoking, but necessity was laid upon me—
the word of God, I thought, ought to be considered first.   And I said to myself, go I must
to all who appear to be wise that I may find
out the meaning of the oracle.   And I swear
to you, Athenians, the result of my mission
was this, just this : I found the men most in
repute were all but the most foolish : and
that some inferior men were really wiser and
better.   I went also to the men of letters and
to the men who worked with their hands,
and, after labours that I may well call
herculean, I came at last to find that the

god was true though every man should be a liar.   Now this investigation which has been laid upon me has led to my having many enemies of the worst and most dangerous kind; it has also given occasion to a multitude of calumnies.   But, O men of Athens, God only is wise : all the wisdom of the wisest man is foolishness before God.   And when He spake to Chærephon of Socrates, He did not mean *me* : He only used my name by way of illustration : as if He had said, He, O Men, is the wisest of the Greeks, who, like Socrates, knows that his wisdom is in truth worth nothing.   And so I have gone on my way, obedient to the god, and have made inquisition into the wisdom of every one, citizen or stranger, who appears to be wise ; and it is my duty to the oracle to show him that he is not wise : and this, the one occupation of my life, has wholly absorbed me, so that I have had no time to give to any other public interest or to any private concern of my own : and now in old age and utter poverty I am at your bar on trial for my life—and all by reason of my devotion to the god."

Such is Socrates' own account of his divine

call to the philosophical apostleship, an apostleship which he pursued in season and out of season among his fellow-townsmen for the next thirty years. For from that day Socrates gave up everything to the fulfilment of his sacred task of teaching all men the true wisdom as it had been revealed to himself. Morning, noon, and night, he was henceforth to be found mingling with the men of the city, enquiring, conversing, debating, cross-questioning; no figure was so well known to the Athenians of that generation as that of Socrates, and no figure was so striking, not to say startling, as his. He was of middle height, of herculean strength, and, to the end of his life, he enjoyed the most splendid health; but with all this his was the most uncomely figure that was ever seen on the streets of a Greek city. His face was the standing jest of his enemies, while his admiring friends were wont to contrast the divine beauty of his soul with the grotesque ugliness of his countenance. His broad flat nose, with its turned-up nostrils, his negro-like lips, and his bulging-out lobster-like eyeballs; and, latterly, his Falstaffian stomach, which grew the grosser the more he starved himself

—all this, with his ragged cloak and his
unsandalled feet, combined to make up a
picture that not even Aristophanes' mask-
maker could caricature. From early morning, through all the hours of every day, that
uncouth figure was to be seen rolling about
with a more than Johnsonian love of the
streets of the city and of all the crowded
haunts of men. In the market-place, among
the booths of the greengrocers and the tables
of the money-changers, at the baths and in
the playgrounds, in the schools and in the
workshops, Socrates spent the livelong day
talking, as he had opportunity, to all men—
to rich and poor, to statesmen and trades-
men, to learned and simple, full to all of
jest and good humour, kind to all, afraid of
none — the friend and counsellor of the
young and inexperienced, but the mortal
enemy of the proud, the pretentious, and the
self-conceited. " Socrates was the first philosopher," says Diogenes, " who conversed continually about human life " ; and one who
daily heard him and took a memorandum
of what he said, thus sums up his master's
conversations : " He spake only of what it
most concerned all men to know : he was

always considering what was pious and what was impious in human life and character. What was becoming, and what was unbecoming : what was just, and what was unjust : what was sanity, and what was insanity : what was fortitude, and what cowardice : what a State was, and what the true character of a statesman : dwelling always on the things it most concerned men to know and practise, seeking continually to deliver men from ignorance, and slavery and vice. With infinite skill he turned every conversation he took part in to practical uses ; to intellectual and moral and religious ends. Socrates' ruling passion, the one thing he determined to teach and practise, as he perambulated the streets of his native city, compelling all men's attention, was this : ' One thing is needful, enter into thyself : examine thyself : know thine own ignorance : above all other knowledge, *know thyself.*' "

Nor are we left with short summaries and dry abstracts of the conversations of the sage. Plato has placed us in his everlasting debt by delivering into our eager hands whole volumes of detailed dialogues, complete diaries, day after day, of his master's dis-

courses. As I have already said, the reporter here is so much a man of genius that
we must take Plato with Socrates, the
scholar with the master; they can never
henceforth be separated. At the same time,
for our purpose, Socrates speaks with sufficient force and individuality in every Dialogue of his disciple. Take as an illustration
the delightful drama of the *Lysis*, in which
Socrates when an old man discourses with a
group of young lads about their youthful
friendships and dawning loves. It is like a
breath of morning air to be taken into the
beautiful new park outside the city gates,
and hear the kind old man talking with such
sweet banter, and with so much true wisdom,
to the young men who gathered round him.
Socrates did not act as if that subject which,
above all other subjects, is near a young
man's heart, nearer than wrestling and running, shooting and fishing, was a guilty
secret : a lover in his eyes was not a criminal
or a fool ; and, accordingly, he often found
opportunity of getting at a young man's
deepest thoughts, and of conferring with
him and advising him as if he had still been
a young man himself. " O Hippothales,"

he cried to a blushing youth, " do not say that you are, or that you are not, in love : the confession is too late : for I see not only that you are in love : but that you are already far gone in your love. Simple and foolish as I am, the gods have given me the eyes to see the signs of this secret malady." And as from that he went on and discoursed and debated about the love of parents and children, brothers and sisters, schoolboys and men : of what creates affection, and what feeds it, and what starves it : what strains it, and what repairs it, and what wholly and irrecoverably kills it — the lads left their games and came and sat around the old man's knee. They were just in the thick of these topics when their tutors appeared on the scene and summoned them home. " O Menexenus and Lysis, I cried after them at parting, how ridiculous that you two boys, and I, an old boy who would fain be one of you, should talk so much about friendship and affection, and yet not be able, as we have not been, to say really what it is that constitutes a true and abiding friendship." It may well have been that Menexenus and Lysis and their companions could

not correctly report to any one the conversation held in the Palæstra that summer
evening, but all the days of their life they
could not fail to have a clearer head and a
truer heart after their memorable time with
father Socrates.

In a kindred dialogue a headache that
Charmides has every morning gives rise to a
delightful debate in which health of body
and soundness of mind are discoursed over
with true Socratic power. Since intemper-
ance in some form or other is usually at the
bottom of our morning headaches it naturally
comes to be asked what constitutes a true
temperance. First to young Charmides himself that question is put, and then to Critias,
his companion : and as the dialogue goes on
that question is raised and pressed after
Socrates' manner in a multitude of ways till
the notion of temperance is enlarged and
enriched to contain not command of appetite
only, but all kinds of moderation, sobriety,
and balance; all modesty, all decency, all
discretion, all wisdom : till we have clean
forgotten poor Charmides and his morning
headache. But he had this for his consolation that he has given his otherwise unknown

name to one of the most exquisite Dialogues
of Plato : we will always think of him as the
noble-born and handsome youth to whose
slight morning malady we owe the delightful
Charmides.

We have an excellent example of Socrates'
usual process of cross-questioning in his
recorded conversation with Glaucon, a young
parliamentary candidate. Glaucon was the
brother of Plato, and, no doubt, had some
share of the philosopher's great talents, but
he was far too young for public life, and he
was fast making both himself and his friends
ridiculous by his ignorance and presumption.
But nothing would hold him off the platform
till Socrates took him in hand to heckle him,
which he did, according to Xenophon, in this
manner. Stopping him one day in the street
Socrates said to the ambitious youth : " And
so, Glaucon, you are to govern the State for
us ? " " That is my hope," replied the
youth. " By Jupiter," said Socrates, " it is
an honourable office," and then he went on
to extol magistracies and to tell of what
great statesmen and generals had done for
their country, for their families, and for themselves, till the youth's heart was all on fire.

" But it is plain, Glaucon," said Socrates,
" that if you wish to be honoured and rewarded by the State, you must first in
some way benefit the State. "Certainly, certainly," cried Glaucon. " Tell me, then, my
son," said Socrates, "tell me how you
propose to benefit the State. Would you try
to make the State richer?" "Assuredly,"
said Glaucon. " Let us talk then, to begin
with, about the present revenues of the
State. Tell me, for you must know, for you
are a man of affairs, and I am an old stone
polisher, tell me whence the revenues of
Athens chiefly come, and what is their present amount, and, especially, how you propose
to increase them." " These are matters,"
said Glaucon, " I have not yet considered."
" Well, then, do you come to us proposing
any retrenchment on our annual expendi-
ture ? " " Pardon me," said the youth,
" but I have not had time to master all these
matters. But surely it is possible to enrich
the State at the expense of our enemies."
" Extremely possible," replied Socrates, " if
we are stronger than they ; but if we are
weaker we may soon lose all we have. Now
that we may have some idea of our chances

with our enemies let us rapidly go over the strength of the country by land and by sea." " By Jupiter," cried Glaucon, " you do not expect me to carry all these things at my finger-ends." " Well then," said Socrates, " if you have it all written down at home, bring it, and read it to me." " But to tell you the truth," said Glaucon, " I have not yet got it written down." And so on, and so on through all departments of public business, till the ambitious youth was thoroughly turned inside out, when Socrates said to him : " Take care, Glaucon, lest, while you are eager to acquire glory, you meet with the reverse of it. Do you not see how dangerous it is for a person to speak about, and much more to undertake, what he does not understand. If, therefore, you still wish to gain esteem and reputation in the country, endeavour to understand thoroughly what you wish to do." Whether or no Glaucon was from that day to be found among the enemies of Socrates we are not told, but it would depend on what kind of stuff Glaucon was at bottom made of.

The very next chapter of the *Memorabilia* exhibits Socrates in conversation with a man the very opposite of Glaucon. He is described as a man of the highest character, and of far more ability than most of those who were ruling the State, but he hesitated to take to the platform, or to accept any share in the government of the city. A fine public spirit breathes through this whole interview, and Socrates at last brings it to a close with this counsel : " Be not ignorant of yourself, my friend, as to what you can do, and what you cannot do : strive to cultivate to the utmost all your powers, and do not be regardless of the affairs of your own country, if any one department of them can be improved by what you can do."

I find I must pass over Socrates' advice to an embarrassed landlord, and the counsel he gave to two brothers who were quarrelling about the family estate ; and his conversation with his eldest son, Lamprocles, about Xanthippe, his mother's bad temper, and many other things I had intended to tell you, in order to set forth the outline of an argument he once held with an agnostic of that day. Xenophon tells us that he heard the discourse, and Xenophon was not the man either to extend or adorn what Socrates said.

Aristodemus, nicknamed the Little—Apollodorus describes him in the *Symposium* as a
little fellow who never wore any shoes. He
was a perfect worshipper of Socrates—neither
sacrificed to the gods, nor prayed to them,
nor attended to auguries, but despised and
ridiculed every pious person, till one day
Socrates took him in hand. " Tell me,
Aristodemus, do you admire any men for
their genius ? " " Of course I do," said the
dapper little Positivist. " Tell me their
names," said Socrates. Aristodemus gave
him a list commencing, of course, with
Homer in poetry, and closing with Zeuxis
in painting. " And whether do those who
form images without sense or motion, or
those who create living creatures endowed
with sense and vital energy, appear to you
most worthy of admiration ? " With which
question Socrates launched the conversation
into the very heart of the argument from
final causes, anticipating our English Paley's
beautiful book by three and twenty centuries.
"However, Socrates," said Aristodemus, "you
must understand that I do not despise
the gods, I only consider them to be too
exalted to need my attention." " But,"

said Socrates, " the more exalted they are, while they deign to attend to you, the more you ought to honour them." " Be assured," said Aristodemus, " that if I believed the gods took any thought for men, I would not neglect them." To which Socrates replies with a long and impressive argument for the fatherly Providence of Almighty God, winding up with this challenge : " What more must God do before you will believe that He cares for you ? " " I will think so," said the stout little sceptic, " when He sends to me, as you say He sends to you, monitors to show me what I ought, and what I ought not to do." To which Socrates made answer, almost in the very words of a greater than he to the cavillers of another nation, and another day : " If any man will do His will, he shall know the doctrine, whether it be of God."

Before leaving this part of my subject I must take leave to introduce you to Agathon's hospitable banquet-hall, if only to let you see Socrates in a new character, and at the same time to let you hear a sample of the table-talk of an Athenian supper party in the fifth century B.C.

One afternoon Aristodemus, our little

agnostic friend, was passing the door of
the bath when, who should come out but
Socrates, sandalled and perfumed to the
utter surprise, not to say offence, of his
somewhat austere disciple. " Where are you
bound for to-day, so finely got up " ? asked
Aristodemus. " To a banquet at Agathon's,"
replied Socrates ; " he is giving a feast of
several days' duration for a tragic victory he
has lately won. I was asked yesterday, but
I put off till to-day when the crowd will not
be so great ; I am now on my way, and I
have put on my best, as you see, because
Agathon is rather particular about these
things. But come along with me," said
Socrates, putting his hand into the arm of
the little unsandalled man, " Agathon is
not such a snob as not to make any friend
of mine welcome at any time, and in any
array." Aristodemus could never resist the
temptation of being near Socrates, which
leads us to hope that at last he may have
attained to his master's faith. And together
they went toward Agathon's door. But
Aristodemus arrived there without his proper
introductions. For, as often happened with
Socrates, a thoughtful fit came on him by

the way, which fixed him to the spot, and nothing would ever move or interest him as long as the fit lasted. "Welcome," said Agathon, "but what have you made of Socrates ? " A servant was sent out to look for the missing guest, who came back and reported that Socrates was standing stock-still under the portico of a neighbouring house, and would neither hear nor speak, so taken up was he with his own thoughts. Supper went on, and still no Socrates, but at last he appeared at the door, when Agathon rose and led him to a seat beside himself, saying jokingly that he would like to be within touch of Socrates in hope of getting the benefit of that wise thought that had come to him in the portico and which had nearly cost him his supper. "How I wish," said Socrates, taking his place as desired, "How I wish that wisdom could be infused by touch, out of the fuller into the emptier man : in that case how much I should prize sitting by you, Agathon. For you would have filled me full of wise and beautiful things, in comparison with which mine are of a very mean and questionable kind, indeed no better than a dream : but your ability is bright and only beginning, as was manifested forth only yesterday in the presence of thirty thousand applauding Hellenes." "You are mocking me," said Agathon: "ere long you and I will have to settle who is to bear the palm of wisdom : but for the present you are behind with your supper." After the cloth was removed, a hymn was sung, and a libation offered to heaven ; and then, instead of a night of all-round compulsory drinking, as last night had been, it was resolved that the Symposium should be spent in rational conversation. "If you agree with me," said Eryximachus, a learned physician who formed one of the company, "there will be no lack of conversation ; for I mean to propose that each of us shall in turn make an oration in honour of Love, and let us have the very best that can be made." "No one will vote against that proposal," said Socrates, "for myself, this is the only subject on which I profess to have any knowledge. Nor can Agathon or Pausanias refuse to speak : and there can be no doubt of Aristophanes, who is the constant servant of Dionysus and Aphrodite. But let Phædrus begin, and good luck to him ! "

And thus began a Symposium of wit and
wisdom the like of which the world has never
again seen : for this Symposium had Love for
its theme ; Socrates for its chief speaker ;
Aristophanes for its fool ; and Plato for its
reporter. Through the livelong night the
wine flowed, but the wit and wisdom out-
flowed the wine, till we have a dialogue in
which Plato excels himself. To say to anyone who has never opened Plato that the
Symposium treats of love conveys to him
nothing : or rather, it conveys the most
misleading of ideas. To mention " love " to
nine persons out of ten is to degrade and
defile the noblest word of human speech : but
if ever love were worthily treated of outside
the New Testament it was on that brilliant
night at Agathon's supper-table. " The
power of love," says Jowett in his exquisite
Introduction, " is represented in the Symposium as running through all nature and all
being : at one end descending to animals and
plants, and attaining to the highest vision
of truth at the other. In an age when man
was seeking for an expression of the world
around him, the conception of love greatly
affected him. . . . Love became a mythic

personage, whom philosophy, borrowing from poetry, converted into an efficient cause of creation. . . . In the Symposium love is not merely the feeling usually so called, but the mystical contemplation of the beautiful and the good." The highest love is not the love of any earthly person : the highest love is the love of heaven. The unity of truth, the enthusiasm for knowledge, the faith in the invisible, and the adoration of the Eternal all entered into the table-talk on the subject of Love at that immortal Symposium.

But, if only to show you how universal is the sad proverb that " a prophet is not without honour, save in his own country, and in his own house," I will now ask you to accompany me on a short visit to the Theatre of Athens. The *Clouds* of Aristophanes, one of the most brutally riotous of his many brutal performances, is to-day to be put on the boards, and thousands are crowding to take their places in the vast arena. That the best man Athens has ever seen is to be bespattered and caricatured and tossed among the feet of the ignorant mob only fills the enormous house the fuller. When the curtain rises the scene is laid in the bedroom of Strepsiades, a

countryman near Athens. He is seen tossing
about in bed and swearing by Jupiter that
the sun will not rise though the cocks have
been crowing for hours. He has not slept a
wink all night so tormented has he been by
the enormous debts his spendthrift son has
contracted on the turf. At last the prodigal
also wakens, and a colloquy ensues between
father and son so clever that it might have
taken place to-day between any demented old
father among ourselves and his gambling son.
The old man will not pay the debts of his
son, and yet he cannot get out of them—and
what is to be done ? At last he bethinks himself of "The Wisdom-shop"—subtilty-shop,
where he has been told dishonest debtors are
taught how to bamboozle their creditors, and,
right or wrong, to gain their causes with
the judge. And the first scene closes with
father and son setting out to seek the
advice of Socrates in the Wisdom-shop. The
second scene shows the inside of Socrates'
School—he kept no school, but truth is not
one of Aristophanes' many talents—where
his scholars are engaged on such studies as
only the riotous imagination of Aristophanes
could invent : while the master himself is

seen swinging in a basket, far above the heads
of his scholars, in contemplation of heavenly
mysteries.

> "Come down, sweet Socrates, and teach me quickly
>   The knowledge of those things for which I came."
>   "What camst thou for ? "
> "To learn the art of speaking.
>   With debts and usury I'm torn in pieces,
>   Tossed up and down, and forced to pawn my goods.
>   By horses eaten into this consumption :
>   And I would learn of you that language,
>   Which teaches men to pay nothing ; for which,
>   By all the gods, I'll pay you what you ask."

The old man then puts his spendthrift
son to Socrates' school : but instead of
learning there to hoodwink his creditors he
only learns greater insolence toward his aged
father : and, in short, the wisdom-shop only
finishes what the betting-office has begun.
And so mischievous and selfish a part does
Socrates play in the domestic trouble that
at last the exasperated father and the black-
guard son both turn against Socrates : and
the last scene of the long comedy sees the
" Wisdom-shop " in flames, and Socrates
smothered among the ruins.   We   need
Aristophanes, with his libels and brutalities,
to account to us for the fact that Socrates

was so often assailed and maltreated on the
public street : and, but for the light the great
comedian throws on that time, the indictment
and trial and execution of Socrates would
have been too great an enigma to us. For to
that trial, and the tragedy that followed it,
we must now come.

For thirty years Socrates had been allowed
to go about his great work, if not altogether
unmolested, yet with only such attacks as
Aristophanes had made on him in the theatre,
and such assaults as he had suffered from
the mob on the street. His worst enemies,
who were working behind the comedian and
behind the crowd, had not yet dared to
strike openly at Socrates ; but at last their
enmity came to a head, and they determined
to risk all on a public prosecution. And thus
it came about that one day when Socrates
came abroad to commence his public ministry
he saw an ominous handwriting affixed to
the Archon's porch, and going up to it he
read what he had been long looking for :
" Socrates, the son of Sophroniscus, is im-
peached, inasmuch as he does not believe in
the gods the city worships, but introduces
other strange deities ; he is also guilty,

inasmuch as he corrupts the young men :
and the punishment he has incurred is
death." This is not to be a common criminal
trial : this is to be at once a criminal trial,
a political impeachment, and a religious prosecution. The indictment has been drawn
so as to leave no possible chance of escape :
for it gathers up all the grudges, it concen-
trates all the enmities, it inflames all the
superstitions, and it invokes all the fears of
an angry city. Heaven and earth : the home
and the temple : the gods and men are all
to be invoked against the aged Socrates.
The trial took place before a jury of 501
Athenian citizens, with a crowd of spec-
tators gathered around. There is only one
other trial that stands before the trial of
Socrates in interest to us : but that is a
trial which is not to be named beside any
trial of the sons of men.

Absorbing as everything connected with
the trial of Socrates is, yet, all our interest is
drunk up by the report of Socrates' defence
of himself which Plato has preserved to us.
All I have said about Plato as a reporter of
Socrates applies in its fullest force to the
Apology : but the gift Plato here puts into

our hands is so precious that we feel it almost an impiety to raise any critical questions concerning it.   I wish I could read the whole of the *Apology* to you.   You must all read it sometime for yourselves.

After all Socrates' accusers had been heard, the aged sage rose up and addressed his judges as follows : " How you, O Athenians, have been affected by my accusers, I cannot tell : but I know that they made me almost forget myself—so persuasively did they speak —and yet they have hardly uttered one word of truth : but you shall hear from me ' the truth, the whole truth, and nothing but the truth ' : and that, too, in such a shape as occurs to me at the moment.   I am more than seventy years old : and I appear now before a criminal court for the first time— bear with me then, if I am a stranger to the forms that are observed here."   After this exordium Socrates went on to show how persistently public opinion had been poisoned against him by a host of secret enemies— " whose names," he says, " I do not even know, and cannot tell : unless in the chance case of a comic poet."   And then, taking up the thought he felt sure was in many minds

—that such charges must have some foundation, Socrates goes on to narrate his call to
the philosophical life—a narration I have
already given in an earlier part of this paper.
He then takes up the charge that is laid
against him of corrupting the youth : the
utter preposterousness of which he has no
difficulty in making manifest. But instead
of attempting to follow him through the
great argument of the *Apology*, let me rather
quote some golden sentences out of it to
show you what the man Socrates was when
thus in the clutches of his enemies.

" I have said enough," he goes on, " to
answer the charge of Meletus : any elaborate
defence is unnecessary : but I know that I
have many enemies, and this is what will be
my destruction if I am destroyed : of that I
am certain : not Meletus, my accuser, nor
Anytus, but the envy and detraction of the
world, which has been the death of many
good men, and will probably be the death of
many more : there is no danger of my being
the last of them. But some will say, Are
you not ashamed Socrates, of a course of
life which is likely to lead you to an untimely
end ? To him I may fairly answer, There you

are mistaken : a man who is good for anything ought not to calculate the chances of living or dying : he ought only to consider whether what he is doing is right or wrong : whether he is acting the part of a good man or a bad. . . . Wherever a man's true place is there he ought to remain in the hour of danger : he should not for one moment fear death, or, indeed, anything but wrong-doing and disgrace. . . . Men of Athens, I honour and love you : but I shall obey God rather than you : and while I have life and strength I shall never cease exhorting every one I meet and saying unto him : ' O my friend, why do you, who are a citizen of the great and mighty and wise City of Athens, care so much about laying up the greatest amount of money and honour and reputation, and all the time care so little about wisdom and truth and the greatest improvement of the soul ? Are you not ashamed of the life you lead ? '—Thus I go about doing nothing else but persuading you all not to take so much thought for your persons and properties, but first and chiefly to seek the improvement of the soul. This is my teaching, and if this corrupts the youth then my influence is ruinous indeed. . . . And now to you and to God I commit my cause, to be determined by you as is best for you and me." And then, when the vote was taken, and it was found to have gone against him, and he was again permitted to speak—turning to those who had voted death to him, he said: "And now, O men who have condemned me, I would fain prophesy to you : for I am about to die, and that is the hour in which men are gifted with prophetic power. Me you have killed because you wanted to do wrong and escape the accuser : to live ill and yet not to have to give an account of your ill lives. But that will not be possible for you : far otherwise . . . if you think that by killing men you can keep all censure off your evil lives, you are fatally mistaken : that is not the way of escape that is either possible or honourable. The easiest and noblest way is not by disabling others, but by improving yourselves." And turning to those who had acquitted him the aged sage said : " O Judges, be of good cheer about death, and know of a certainty, that no evil can happen to a good man, either in life or after death. He and his are not neglected by God : nor has my own approaching end happened by mere chance. . . . And now, the hour of my departure has arrived, and we go our ways—I go to die, and you to live. Which is better God only knows."

After his trial and sentence Socrates lay in irons for thirty days waiting his execution. During these thirty days a great state solemnity was in progress, and till it was finished it was not lawful to put any Athenian citizen to death : during the holy month the city could not be polluted with blood. But at last the sacred ship arrived from Delos, and the day dawned which was to be Socrates' last day on earth. The inner circle—the Peter and James and John of the Socratic discipleship—are early gathered into Socrates' cell. By Plato's affectionate and eloquent pen we see the whole scene. We see Socrates sitting on the side of his pallet-bed, with an admiring, indeed, an almost worshipping, circle around him. "I had a singular feeling in being in his company that fatal morning," says Phædo. "For I could not bring myself to pity him : his bearing and his language were so noble and so fearless in the hour of death that he appeared to me to be already among the blessed. And indeed so happy was he, and so much himself, he made us all forget where we were : we were all laughing and weeping by turns."

After the jailer had taken the irons off Socrates' leg he changed his position on the bed, and rubbing his galled foot, began to discourse on the mysteries of pleasure and pain as they chase each other through this mortal frame, just as if he had been debating at Agathon's supper-table, or talking to Lysis in the summer-garden. And then, giving a turn to the conversation as was his wont, he said : " but as I am soon going to another place, I ought to be thinking and talking of the nature of the pilgrimage I am about to take. What can I do better between this and the setting of the sun ? "

And then he talked of death, and of a man's due preparation for it. As he talked, Crito, one of his most intimate friends, came up to him and told him that the prison attendant whose office it was to give him the hemlock cup was afraid that he was talking too much and exciting himself so that the poison might not act, and that he might have

to drink it two or three times. " Then," said
Socrates, " let the man mind his business, and
be prepared to give the poison twice or even
thrice if necessary : that is all," and resumed
the conversation. And thus the day passed,
the full record of which may be read in the
Phædo of Plato.

At last the shadows began to lengthen and
the old jailer came in with the hemlock cup
in his hand, when, bursting into tears, he
begged his prisoner's forgiveness, and said to
him : " You know my errand." " See," said
Socrates to those around him, " see how
charming the man is. Since I have been in
the prison he has always been coming unto
me ; at times he would talk with me, and
now see how he sorrows for me. Come, my
friend," he said to the jailer, " you are experienced in such things, come, and give me
my directions how I shall proceed."

The man answered, " You have only to
walk about till your limbs are heavy, and
then to lie down, and the poison will act."
And so saying, he handed the cup to Socrates.
" Taking the cup in his easiest and gentlest
manner," says Phædo, " he looked at the
jailer with all his eyes, and said : ' What do

you say about my making a libation out of
this cup ? ' The man answered, ' We only
prepare, Socrates, just as much as we deem
enough.' ' I understand,' said Socrates, ' but
that need not hinder me from asking the gods
to prosper my journey—and so be it according to my prayer!' Then, holding the cup
to his lips, quite readily and cheerfully he
drank the hemlock. Socrates was now the
only calm man in all the prison. ' What is
all this outcry for ? ' he asked. ' Be quiet,
and let a man die in peace.' When we heard
that we were ashamed, and refrained our
tears : and he walked about, we watching
him, till his strength began to fail, and the
cold crept up into his heart, when he lay down.
The dying man then covered his face with his
mantle, and soon was no more. Such was the
end of our friend, whom I may truly call the
wisest, and justest, and best of all the men
whom I have ever known."

III

Though I have not yet spoken of the
Dæmon of Socrates, or as we may call it his
Good Angel, do not suppose that I have

forgotten it. Far from that : for I have
been in its presence and under its power all
the evening, as I shall now in closing show
you. But what, exactly, was the Dæmon
of Socrates ? This has been a debated
question among the students of Plato and
Xenophon from their day to ours : and the
latest writers on Socrates, such as Zeller and
Grote, and Riddell, and Jowett, still debate
the question, and leave its solution open. It
would be too presumptuous in me to attempt
to enter the lists of philosophical debate
among such men : but, perhaps, I may be
allowed to say here, and for myself, that I
have no doubt in my own mind at all as to
what Socrates' Dæmon really was: and I
shall take up my remaining time in putting
that interesting and important subject somewhat fully before you.

To begin at the beginning :—The Greek
word δαίμων, degraded into our *demon*, was
used by the Greeks to denote either a god, or
some being partaking more or less in the
divine nature. But the name δαίμων had
always this distinction and limitation about
it that it invariably denoted such a being in
his relations to men. We are fortunate, in

this connection, that we have in one place
Socrates' own explanation of the name, or,
if not Socrates', then Plato's, which is perhaps
better. Among the many etymologies that
are discussed in the Cratylus, that of δαίμων
also comes up. " I wish," says Socrates to
Hermogenes, the grammarian, " I wish that
you would consider what is the real meaning
of this word ' dæmons.' I wonder whether
you would think my view right." " Let me
hear it," said Hermogenes. " You remember
how Hesiod uses the name," said Socrates ;
" speaking of what he calls a ' golden race of
men who came first,' he says of them :

" But now that fate has closed over this
race they are holy dæmons upon the earth,
beneficent, averters of ills, guardians of
mortal men." " And," adds Socrates, " I
have the most entire conviction that Hesiod
called those departed men dæmons, because
they were δαίμονες (knowing or wise), as the
gods are—and in this ancient Attic dialect
this is the very form of the word. . . . And
I hold with him, Hermogenes, and I say too
that every wise and good man is more than a
man, both in life and in death, and is rightly
called a dæmon, or the dwelling-place of a

dæmon." "I believe," replies Hermogenes, "that I quite agree with you in that."

So much for the unusual name. Let us now enquire of Xenophon what he has to tell us about the Dæmon that was always counselling with his master. "It was a common subject of talk," says Xenophon, "that Socrates used to say that the divinity, τὸ δαιμόνιον, instructed him." "He also told his friends about him to do many things, intimating that the δαίμων had forewarned him, and that they would repent who disregarded the δαίμων." And it will be remembered that when he was arguing with the sceptic Aristodemus, that clever little man replied : "When the gods send me a Monitor, as you say they send to you, telling me what I ought to do, and what I ought not, then I will think that they care for me." And when one of his friends upbraided Socrates for not preparing a more elaborate defence, and also for saying things in his defence that could not but provoke his judges, Socrates answered, "Of a truth when I set to work to think out my speech, the Dæmon rose up within me and hindered me," or, as it might be translated, "the Dæmon testified his disappro-

bation." And summing up his master's
character, Xenophon says : " So pious was
he that he did nothing without the sanction
of the gods," conveyed to him through the
Dæmon.

Now, though the Dæmon, whatever it was,
frowned on some things Socrates was preparing to put into his Apology, yet, happily,
it did not stop his mouth from speaking about
itself. For, when explaining and account-
ing for his extraordinary life, he went on to
say that the cause of it all was his call by
the oracle, and, along with that, a Voice
that was ever present with him, a certain
emanation from God, a "somewhat divine,"
which his enemies, he complained, had blas-
phemously caricatured and put into the
indictment. " Now this began with me," he
adds, " from my childhood : a certain voice,
which always, when it comes, turns me aside
from that which I am about to do. It was
this which opposed my mixing in politics, and,
I think, very wisely." And further on he
refers to this subject again : " Hitherto the
Oracle, the Dæmon, which is familiarly about
me, with great frequency has opposed itself,
even in very little things, if I were about to

act in any way not rightly." " I happened," he says in the *Euthydemus*, " to be providentially sitting alone in the Lycæum, and I had it in my mind to be gone. But when I got up to go, the Dæmon came, and I therefore sat down again." Again, in the *Phædrus*, " When I was about to cross the river, the Dæmon came, and I seemed to hear a voice which said to me, that I should not proceed till I had expiated myself, as having in some way offended against God." In the *Alcibiades* also he speaks of a " certain divine hindrance "—a hindrance which is " nothing human "; and in the *Theaetetus*, of the Dæmon which comes to him hindering his intercourse with some men and not with others.

These are the leading passages in Xenophon and Plato in which Socrates' Dæmon is spoken of; and though all those authors who treat of Socrates in ancient times take up the subject of his Dæmon, yet they add nothing of value or importance to what those two great authorities have transmitted to us. Plutarch has an unusually verbose discourse on the Dæmon or " Genius " of Socrates, as he calls it, but there is no new information

in it, and no insight; neither is there in
Diogenes.   It has only been in modern times,
and since the birth of the historical and
critical spirit that this hitherto obscure and
perplexed subject has been treated of as it
deserves.   To read Plutarch on the Dæmon
of Socrates, and then turn to Zeller or Grote
or Riddell or Manning on the same subject
is to pass over into a new intellectual world :
it is like talking with a new race of men.   We
feel as we read as if Socrates in his extraordinary talents and still more extraordinary
character had never been truly understood
or appreciated till now.   Much that Socrates
and Plato saw but in a glass darkly has been
made clear as day to us, and much that
" slept in the ear " of their contemporaries
has been spoken as from the housetops to us.

Not that our best modern philosophers have
either satisfied themselves or one another in
their speculations and explanations about
the Dæmon of Socrates.   Perhaps the best
study that has ever been given to this subject is to be found in an appendix to the late
Mr Riddell of Balliol's edition of the Apology.
After a most scholarly discussion of the passages out of Xenophon and Plato, in which

the Dæmon is referred to, Mr Riddell thus sums up : " Socrates' Dæmon was just ' a quick exercise of a judgment informed by knowledge of the subject trained by experience, and inferring from cause to effect without consciousness of the process. In a mind so purified by temperance and self-knowledge, so single of purpose, and unperturbed by lower aims, and endowed with such powerful natural faculties, the ability to forecast and forejudge might become almost an immediate sense.' " True and admirable as Riddell's analysis and estimate is, so far as it goes, I cannot think that it goes far enough. Incomplete as our information is about the Dæmon of Socrates, yet I cannot but think that we are told some things that are not sufficiently recognised in the above explanation. For, let these important points be well kept in mind. The Dæmon was some guide, monitor, divine voice that spoke to Socrates from his youth up : it was a sudden sense as of a divine visitant : it came to him unasked, and it pronounced a judgment, as from God, on his actions; he never disobeyed it, and it grew in strength and clearness till he felt it ever with him; and, lastly, he held that if

other men had it not it was their own fault :
they, too, would have had it, if they had
attended to it, and had obeyed it. Now, it
appears to me that that is as full and as
clear a description of the nature and office of
conscience as we could possibly have had
from a Greek moralist of the fifth century
before Christ. And that too, when we consider that on such a subject as the nature
and functions of the conscience, after all is
said, the observer here was himself inadequate, the reporters incompetent, and then
the record they have left us is necessarily so
imperfect. Even Socrates was not, and at
that day could not be, a sufficiently equipped
observer of what went on within himself.
His conscience was at best but rudimentary
and untaught : those who heard him speak
of the Divine Voice were as much children
in psychology and morality as himself : and
then, the record they have left of his teaching
and his testimony is plainly so occasional
and fragmentary. When all this is fully
considered, to me, the wonder is, that we
have from that land and that day such a
close approximation to our own doctrine and
experience of the Christian conscience. The

more I have read and thought on this subject, the more clear it has become to me that the Dæmon of Socrates was just his conscience personified, hypostatised, as a theologian would say, imaginatively and dramatically thought of by himself and spoken about to others. The full development, evangelical illumination, and true philosophical analysis of the human conscience was not further from his attainment than were many other branches of intellectual and moral and religious truth : but it was Socrates' crowning glory that in that land and at that day he did not speculate as to the nature of the Voice that spake in his heart, but instantly and devoutly obeyed it. And in this, and in the immense impression that this made on the world, Socrates did a service to his own and to all subsequent ages, of infinitely more importance than if he had elaborated a philosophical doctrine of conscience as true to nature and revelation as that we now possess, say, in Butler's immortal Sermons. The student who will be at the trouble to trace the development of the Christian conscience from its rudimentary and natural state in Socrates' Dæmon, up through its supernatural

enlightenment and evangelical enforcement
in Paul, and then pass on to its noble
treatment in Butler and Chalmers and Newman, in whose hands the doctrine takes on
all the keenness and intensity of the flaming
sword itself, will return to Socrates with
renewed wonder at him, and renewed grati-
tude to God, that such knowledge was
granted, and such a life of truth and goodness
was made possible in that heathen dispensation. Socrates told his judges that he had
possessed this inward and divine monitor
from his youth up ; that he had always con-
sulted and obeyed it ; and that even to
please them and purchase their pardon he
could not go against it. He had been taught
by his father and mother that the best way
of worshipping God was to hearken to His
voice and keep all His commandments : and
all his days he had searched and enquired
diligently for that voice as it spake in his
own heart, for he counted it nothing less
than madness in any man not to know his
own heart and not to obey the good and flee
from the evil he found there. " One thing
is needful," he went about continually pro-
claiming, " know thyself : enter into thy-

self." "Know thyself," says Grote in his
great chapter on Socrates, " is the holiest of
all the Socratic texts : it was the text he was
continually citing, and strenuously enforcing
upon all his hearers." We, nowadays, know
" holier " texts than even that, but without
both the knowledge and the practice of that
we shall never know what true holiness is,
nor ever take a single step toward it.   Would
that all Christian men among us, with Paul
and Butler delivering them over to a far
diviner doctrine of conscience than even that
of the Dæmon of Socrates—would that they
all took home to themselves the Socratic
canon, a canon that its noble author for
seventy years both enforced and adorned :
" A human life without constant self-exami-
nation and cross-examination is no true life
at all."

" Drink now," so wrote Diogenes Lærtius
at the end of his famous biography :

Drink now, O Socrates, high in the realm of Jove :
For truly did the God pronounce you wise,
And He who said so is Himself all wisdom :
You drank the poison which your country gave,
But they drank wisdom from your godlike voice.

III

THE NATURE OF ANGELS (I.)

Where the bright Seraphim in burning row
Their loud, uplifted angel-trumpets blow,
And the cherubic host in thousand quires
Touch their immortal harps of golden wires,
With those just Spirits that wear victorious palms,
Hymns devout and holy psalms
Singing everlastingly :
That we on earth with undiscording voice
May rightly answer that melodious noise ;
As once we did, till disproportioned sin
Jarred against nature's chime, and with harsh din
Broke the fair music that all creatures made
To their great Lord, whose love their motion swayed
In perfect diapason, whilst they stood
In first obedience, and their state of good.
O may we soon again renew that song,
And keep in tune with Heav'n, till God ere long
To his celestial concert us unite,
To live with Him, and sing in endless morn of
    light.

JOHN MILTON.

THE NATURE OF ANGELS (I.)

" He took not on him the nature of angels."—HEB ii. 16.
" For unto the angels hath he not put in subjection the
world to come, whereof we speak. But one in a certain
place testified, saying, What is man, that thou art mindful
of him ? or the son of man, that thou visitest him ? Thou
madest him a little lower than the angels ; thou crownedst
him with glory and honour, and didst set him over the
works of thy hands : thou hast put all things in subjection
under his feet. For in that he put all in subjection under
him, he left nothing that is not put under him. But now
we see not yet all things put under him. But we see Jesus,
who was made a little lower than the angels for the suffering
of death, crowned with glory and honour ; that he by the
grace of God should taste death for every man."—HEB.
ii. 5-9.
" Being made so much better than the angels, as he hath
by inheritance obtained a much more excellent name than
they."—HEB. i. 4.

[First given in St George's, Edinburgh, 18th December 1870.]

WHY is there so much made of the angels in
this passage ? Why is there so much space
and quotation and argument expended on
what seems to us a somewhat irrelevant
matter ? Might not the Epistle to the
Hebrews have been greatly condensed and
simplified had the reader's attention been
fixed at once on the Priesthood of Christ,

instead of having to pass through this long introduction concerning angels and Moses which no one disputes, and which does not seem to bring any strength to the great argument of the Epistle ?

A slight reading of the book will suffice to start these questions, but it requires a deeper and harder reading fitly to answer them. And still such a reading will be amply repaid in a more living and intelligent hold of the main theme when we come to it.

The introductory portion of this Epistle is not addressed to mature and well-grounded Christians of the nineteenth century so much as to the immature Jewish converts of the first, who were as yet "unskilful in the word of righteousness, and had need of milk and not of strong meat." They had not yet understood the principles of the doctrine of Christ, they were still exercised about the doctrine of baptism and laying on of hands, about Moses and his Law, and about angels and their place in its dispensation. The Apostle had to become all things to all men, and he knew that there was simply no use plunging at once into the heart of his theme when such obstacles as these lay in the way of his readers following him. Hence he spends several chapters on clearing the path for the weaker brethren, who feared that in going forward with the great Christian movement they were thereby somehow in danger of forsaking the old paths in which their fathers had walked.

But still the question awaits an answer. Why so much in the first and second chapters concerning angels ?

The answer is simply this : the appearances and messages of angels held the place in the Old Testament that the appearance and teaching of Christ do in the New. A light surrender of the old order and the ministry of angels would have revealed but a poor capacity for receiving the new, and these Hebrews with the blood of Abraham and Isaac and Jacob, of Moses and the prophets in their veins would have their childhood steeped in Old Testament narrative concerning the deliverances wrought and the comfort sent by angels : for all down the nation's chequered history their cheering words had been heard and their ministering wing seen.   And, above all, the Angel of the Covenant, the Angel of the Lord, had brought God the Father so near that it might almost be said—they had in him preludes and anticipations of the incarnation itself. It was through his ministry that the patriarchs were called, and led, and prospered : it was through his disposition of the Law that it came into Moses' hands : it was through him that the prophets spoke unto the fathers. God took the form, and came in the character, of an angel when he conveyed anything new or confirmed any old revelation of grace or truth to the Hebrew people. In a word, what the Son is under the New Testament economy, that the ministry of angels was under the Old.

But retrograde and Judaising teachers had played upon the prejudices and the piety of the Hebrew Christians by exalting Moses and the Law that came by the dispensation of angels, and therefore to show that Jesus is rightly counted of more honour than Moses, and that He has by indisputable inheritance a greater than an angelic name, he has undertaken to show that Christ has superseded the ministry of angels in revealing the Father, and has also set aside the stewardship of Moses, being a Son over His own house.

We are now ready to follow the Apostle into this argumentative passage in which he seeks to exalt the dignity of Christ above the angels.

Verse three dwells through several striking clauses on what the Son was, and is, and in His divine nature will ever be, the " brightness of the Father's glory, and the express image of his person, upholding all things by the word of his power." Then comes a clause covering His work on earth : " by himself he purged our sins," and then another stating that He is now " at the right hand of the Majesty on high."

Verse four then accounts for His exaltation, and so carries forward the arguments for this excellent dignity of the risen Redeemer. He has sat down at the right hand of God : " being made so much better than the angels, as he hath by inheritance obtained a more excellent name than they."

This passage was one of the Arian strongholds during the great controversy concerning the eternal Sonship and perfect divinity of the Redeemer. This verse was taken along with the second verse of the third chapter, where it is said that Christ was " faithful to him that appointed or made him," and also, Acts ii. 36, when Peter says : " Therefore let all the house of Israel know assuredly, that God hath made that same Jesus, whom ye have crucified, both Lord and Christ." In those passages, as here, the word " made " plainly occurs concerning the Saviour. And that fact kept these verses like so many disputed provinces which were taken and retaken by Arian and Orthodox till Athanasius finally settled the sense of these texts and put into the great creed that the Son was " begotten not made." But how did he and his followers get over the plain words of the text ? How is the Arian sound shown to contain an orthodox sense ?

In this way and from the plain text of Scripture. The Son who was in the form of God, or, as here, the " express image of his person," and who " thought it no robbery to be equal with God, made himself of no reputation, and took upon him the form of a servant " : the maker of all was made in the likeness of men, being made of a woman, and made under the Law. And being found in fashion as a man, He yet further humbled Himself, and became obedient unto death,

even the death of the Cross.   Wherefore God
hath highly exalted Him, and given Him a
name that is above every name, a more
excellent name than angel ever bore.   For
" at the name of Jesus every knee shall bow,
and every tongue confess that Jesus Christ
is Lord to the Glory of God the Father."

The Arians understood not His generation;
because He was " found in fashion as a man,"
His eternal life was denied.   They staggered
at the grace of the incarnation.   The mystery of godliness, God manifest in the flesh,
was too deep for them.   For remaining what
He was, the eternal Son, He became what
He was not, the Son of Man, and of the seed
of Abraham.   In being made man He " was
made a little lower than the angels," and
those spiritual beings whom He created by
His own power actually came and ministered
unto Him after His temptation in the wilderness, and strengthened Him in His agony in
the Garden.   But though He has thus
emptied Himself, though He has thus for
our salvation become what He was not, still
He necessarily remains what He was, Son of
God.   Conditions change, relations hold.   He
is Son of God made Son of Man ; He is Son

still though Son incarnate, and in a temporary state of suffering and emptiness and humiliation. Here then is a condition of things that makes it plain why Scripture should fearlessly say about its divine Lord, that He was made Lord and Christ, having been " faithful to him that appointed him," that having finished His work the Father raised Him from the dead, and gave Him back His glory, and made Him so much higher than the angels, as he originally, and prior to His humiliation, had a much more excellent name than they.

At the resurrection and exaltation of Christ He was but putting on again that glory He had for our service put off; when He sat down on the right hand of God He was but repossessing Himself of a place and an honour that were inalienably and eternally His own.

But there is more room still for the correct phrase : " made so much better than the angels," for it is not only the Son resuming His suspended honour, and returning to His sonship seat ; but He is returning in a new character, and in a form that shows the Father's grace to be as great in the exaltation of Christ, as the Son's grace was shown to be great in His voluntary humiliation. For the Son is returning to the Father's throne, the Father's bosom, not only divine Son still, but Son of Man in addition. It is a new honour and experience to the Son, and a new display of grace is to realise that He should re-enter to the most excellent glory as a man. It is true the assumption of the human nature into the divine glory in heaven was an easy and a natural thing after its assumption into the Sonship on earth, that drew the rest naturally, necessarily after it. Hence this is no empty apotheosis of a man, but a far more wonderful and gracious work, the incarnation of the Son of God and His subsequent reinstallation into all the Sonship rights and prerogatives. He took our nature, in it purged our sins, and then returned whence He came; went back to the Father with whom He had been before the world was. Thus the exaltation is not of the divine nature only, nor is it a deification of the human only. It is the exaltation of that divine Person who is now God-Man. It is the answer to the Son's prayer. "Glorify thou me with the glory which I had with thee before the world was," before I had emptied myself that I might glorify Thee.

It was a new thing on the earth that the eternal Son of God should tabernacle among men purging their sins ; and it was a new thing in heaven that a Son of Man should appear at the right hand of the Majesty on high.   For this man whom the Jews crucified is assuredly now made Lord Christ.   And He is high above angels as a lord is above his dependents, as the son is above the servants. And they are ever confessing it.   When He had finished the work that was given Him to do, when He had purged our sins, and burst the bonds of death, and blessed His disciples, and sent them to wait on the Spirit's descent, earth had no more work for Him to do.   And He turned His face to His Father's house.   That hour there rang a shout through heaven, the like of which had not been heard there since the morning stars sang together, and the sons of God shouted for joy at the creating work of the eternal Son.

" Lift up your heads, O ye gates : even lift them up ye everlasting doors, and the King of

Glory shall come in!" And as the Son passed in, and ascended to His Father's presence, the angels looking on might have said : " He is preferred before us for He was before us." They had wondered at His surpassing grace when He had passed out into this dark and sinful world ; they worshipped afresh as He passed in again, the Redeemer and Brother of fallen men.

Thus He who had so lately stood in Pilate's judgment hall with a scarlet rag on His shoulders and a crown of thorns on His head, and a reed in His hand, and a crowd of rude men paying Him mock homage till the hour should come to crucify Him, now compels the deep worship of the highest heavens, as He enters with glory as the Lamb that has been slain, having on His vesture and on His thigh a name written more excellent than that of any angel—King of Kings and Lord of Lords.

And a voice was heard in heaven saying : " Sit thou at my right hand until I make thine enemies thy footstool. . . . Thy throne is for ever and ever. . . . Ask of me and I will give thee the heathen for thine inheritance, and the uttermost parts of the earth for thy possession." " And let all the angels of God worship him and wait on his will."

In this marvellous way the eternal Son was " made so much better than the angels as he had by inheritance obtained a much more excellent name than they."

But the Apostle cannot set all this as yet before his Hebrew readers. He has to walk as they are able to follow. He has to argue on premises they already accept, and quote proof and illustration from the Book they read and reverence. Hence he hitches himself to the Old Testament and goes to work to prove by lengthened and full quotation that the Messiah promised there, the Messiah promised to and expected by the fathers, was one who confessedly had a more excellent name than the angels or than Moses. The prophecy that came by the mouth of angels gave to the coming One a name and work far higher than their own. They came and spoke as witnesses and heralds of a greater than any prophet or king who had yet arisen.

Now the Hebrew Christians confessed that Jesus was the Messiah. That all the Mes-

sianic promises and expectations were fulfilled, or were yet to be fulfilled, in Him.
And the Apostle, to disarm their doubt, and
allay their discomfort, about the place the
Old was getting in the triumph of the New,
shows them that the New is the triumph
of the Old; that Jesus who is the Messiah
has simply got that which was promised to
the Messiah. That His name and rank are
higher than the angels that it might be fulfilled that was spoken in Moses and the
fathers and in the prophets concerning Him.
" Come, open your Scriptures," he says, " and
I will show you that that Old Testament
—book and economy—you are so jealous for,
gives such a name and place to the Messiah as
my doctrine gives to Him whom you confess
to be the Messiah."

Hence the long quotations that fill the
page and lay a deep and broad Messianic
foundation for this weighty Epistle. But the
method of proof that an inspired writer drew
out to satisfy the minds and settle the heart
of an ancient Christian, fails, it seems to
satisfy and settle the modern rationalist.
The Apostle's exegesis yields dogmatic results that are distasteful and inadmissible,

and therefore his scholarship, his intelligence, his inspiration, and even his literary honesty are boldly questioned and impugned. And the narrow irrational canon is laid down even by theological teachers that we are to " read Scripture and quote it like any other book."

If this is admitted of course there is an end, if not of religious sentiment and moral duty, at least of all defined and trustworthy theology, as well as much of the peculiar edification and comfort got from Holy Scripture. The believer and the rationalist thus part company at the very threshold of the question. The Christian cannot read Scripture as he reads another book, because for him no other book can claim such an author, as no other book raises such questions, or claims or commands such a hearing. As the Book itself says : " The letter killeth, but the Spirit giveth life." A literal, rationalistic interpretation kills all life out of the Psalms and Prophets, just as a devout and spiritual reading getteth life and giveth it.

Many questions connected with the principles on which New Testament writers quote from and allude to the Old are raised and

discussed in view of this passage before us.
But they are more suited to the study and
the class-room than to the pulpit. Still,
before looking at these quotations in passing, it may be useful to some to say a word
on the general relation that holds between
the first volume of Holy Scripture and the
second. Between the Psalms and Prophets
on the one hand, and the Gospels and
Epistles on the other.

There is nothing in the literary history of
the world at all to compare with the Bible
viewed purely on its literary side. A suc-
cession of writers has arisen for many genera-
tions of men and in lands far separated in
place and circumstance from each other, and
produced a book with beginning, middle, and
end : a book which is one in plan and doctrine, and aim and spirit, though it deals
with the most difficult and lofty questions,
and though scholars, and poets and orators,
craftsmen and fishermen and ploughmen have
contributed to its contents. Take it at the
close of any of its divisions, at the close of
the Pentateuch, at the close of the Psalms,
at the close of the Prophets—the book is
complete ; but it is as a seed or a bud is

complete. It is perfect for its stage, but its stage is one of growth and maturity.

Read Moses and the Prophets and you cannot fail to see that the Old Testament is one in this, that whoever is the writer or the speaker, the spirit of the book, the attitude of the religious life, is one of expectancy and outlook.

The old stands ever on tiptoe looking for the rising of the new; holding forth empty hands, empty but for the typical washing they celebrate, and the prophetic words they hold. They rejoice in God and in what He has done, but they feel that His best waits to be done, and they rejoice with the chastened joy of sojourners and strangers who feel that without us they are not to be made perfect. On one page the Prophet is so lifted up in hope and faith that a thousand years are as one day : he seems to see the day of the Lord and his hope is made glad ; turn it and a day of sorrow has fallen, and he is crying: " How long, O Lord ! How long ! "

The Messianic prophecies are like the garden of the Lord, but it is early summer there : it is rich with buds and blossoms, it is not yet the time of fruit-bearing. The day of the Lord comes and the buds burst in His presence. The fulness of time has brought the fulfilling of prophecy and the unlocking of the type. And still the Book must be read according to its own laws, and not as another book. Even when prophecy is fulfilled and the antitype has come, still he is found to speak another language than the wise men and princes of this world know. He still speaks in words which the Holy Ghost teacheth, which are to one man foolishness, to another the wisdom of God, because by Him they were spiritually discovered. " Open thou mine eyes, O God, that I may behold wondrous things out of thy Law."

The New Testament preacher or writer may be not unfitly likened to a man thinking or writing in a language he is both learning and adding to as he writes. In the construction of an argument like this the Apostle is like one seeking a fit word to clothe his thought so as to place both before his readers. Yea, the thought will not shape itself aright till the right word comes; till the old figure and illustration is found that at once embodies it fully and sheds light on it clearly. As he recalls and sets down in order those quotations, he knows that they will set forth with authority as well as perspicacity what is struggling in his mind. This habit of leaning on the past, and drawing strength from it, even when they were going far beyond it, is as characteristic of the prophets as it is of the apostles. David and Isaiah are the scholars of Moses : quote from, expound, and apply him, just as our Apostle here quotes and applies them. And the books then appear as at once grafted on, and growths out of one another.

To change the figure—the rich golden threads of Messianic prophecy are visible from the beginning of the web though they do not find their end and design till the figure rises in the middle of the work into which they enter, to be lost in its wealth and beauty. And the Apostle here but traces some of the brightest and strongest of such threads up through the loom to prove that the original design had contemplated and made provision for such a central figure.

He is but in his way doing what Christ Himself did when teaching the reluctant disciples concerning the old intention of His suffering and His glory, He said to them:

" These are the things I said unto you while I was yet with you, that all things must be fulfilled which were written in the law of Moses, and in the Prophets, and in the Psalms concerning Me." " Thus opened He their understanding that they might understand the Scriptures."

And thus the Apostle is opening the understanding of the Hebrew Christians to the Messiahship of Jesus and the Sonship of both. For He who was eternal Son, when He had purged our sins, sat down again at the right hand of God. Being made so much better than the angels as He had by inheritance, and even by Jewish prophecy, a much more excellent name than they—" For," he goes on to quote from the Hebrew Scriptures, " For to which of the angels said the Father at any time, 'Thou art my Son, this day have I begotten Thee?'" Now He said this to the Messiah in prophecy.

And again, when the Father bringeth the Firstbegotten into the world He saith: " He maketh his angels spirits and his ministers a flame of fire." And again, quoting from the great Messianic Psalms, the Apostle proves that the coming One is then addressed as possessing just such royal dignity and state as Jesus is now advanced to. Indeed, we search in vain in the historical and doctrinal books of the New Testament for a richer and more exact statement of the Son's glory and reward than we find here in a prophetic psalm concerning the Messiah. " Thy throne, O God, is for ever and ever; a sceptre of righteousness is the sceptre of thy Kingdom. Thou hast loved righteousness and hated iniquity, therefore God, even thy God, hath anointed thee with the oil of gladness above thy fellows."

The psalm from which he quotes next is not usually looked on as properly a messianic psalm, but he finds language there that he knows his readers must admit to be applicable to the Son, as he and they are at one that the Son created the worlds : " Thou Lord in the beginning hast laid the foundation of the earth, and the heavens are the works of thy hands : they shall perish, but thou remainest : and they all shall wax old as doth a garment; and as a vesture worn out, and to be laid aside, shalt thou fold them up, and they shall be changed : but thou art the same, and thy years shall not fail ! "

In a word, to come back to the original thought, "To which of the angels has the Father said at any time, ' Sit on my right hand till I make thine enemies thy footstool?'" The question more than answers itself, for confessedly they are but ministering spirits sent forth from the Son's throne to minister to those He has redeemed, to those who are to be heirs of salvation.

Of this argument and proof, this, then, is the sum : He is Son, in His incarnation and exalted state, Son of God, and angels are His ministers and messengers.

By these quotations and references the Apostle proves what he has advanced above —that the Son is higher than the highest of creatures, better by so much as His inherited name was better than theirs. He is Son and heir ; they are servants and ministers of His.

But His name has an excellency above that of inheritance. He inherits a great name from His Father, but He adds fresh glory to His name as the ages roll on.

He is Son by nature, but He is Creator and Redeemer. He is the Messiah of the Old Testament and the Jesus of the New, a

sacrifice on earth and a great High Priest in
heaven. By grace He has won those names
as by His sword alone, and added them to
that of Son. But that original, inherited
name is the ground and basis of all, just as
His divine nature underlies His human, and
all that in it He performs. He went forth
as Son to make all things ; He was set forth
as Son to inherit man. As Son of God He
came forth from the Father to be the brightness of His glory and the express image of
His person, and as Son of God and Son of
Man He himself purged our sins. But in all
these He got Him glory, and now He has a
name written so full, so deep, so rich with
gracious significance that hitherto no man
knoweth it but He Himself. But that rich
name He now bears will be opened up and
put on the lips of His people when they are
finally with Him to behold His eternal glory
as Son and His added glory as Saviour. But
meantime His excellent name grows as His
work grows, and as His heirship falls in. As
in our names, a new syllable added may be
to the initiated a hint of a whole family
history. An ancestry of wealth and honour
may be claimed and conceded, and a rich

inheritance held by a few letters added to a personal name. Thus ancient names are not seldom made up of fragments of history: they are badges of rank, and signs of heirship and possession. Thus it is that when He shall in heaven or on earth have finished the work His Father and His brethren have given Him to do, He is to be brought forth to the eyes of His people and is to be greeted by the names Faithful and True, not indeed for the first time, but for the first time in all their fulness and warmth on our lips; and on His head shall be many crowns, and He shall have a name written that no man has hitherto known but He himself:

Jesus, my Lord! I know His name,
His name is all my boast:
Nor will He put my soul to shame,
Nor let my hope be lost.
Then will He own His servant's name
Before His Father's face:
And in the New Jerusalem
Appoint my soul a place.

The full knowledge of His name is too wonderful for you. The deep things hidden in it are past finding out. Your heart loses the awful thrill that runs through it as you hear that He is the brightness of His Father's glory, and the express image of His person, but surely your sin and need will not let you forget what the Angel of the Lord said to Joseph : " Thou shalt call his Name Jesus, for he shall save his people from their sins."

IV

THE NATURE OF ANGELS (II.)

Before Him come the choirs of angels, with every principality and power ; the Cherubim with many eyes, and winged Seraphim, who veil their faces as they shout exultingly the hymn.   Alleluia.

From the Liturgy of S. James

THE NATURE OF ANGELS (II.)

"For unto the angels hath he not put in subjection the world to come . . . . "—Heb. ii. 5-9.

[First given in St George's, Edinburgh, 15th January 1871.]

WE come in these verses on one of those frequent quotations from the Old Testament which all but overlay the original text in the opening of the Epistle to the Hebrews. Out of the fourteen verses of the first chapter, nine are quotations from the Psalms, and the body of our text to-day is borrowed from the same book. In modern authorship a quotation is made to give authority or strength or clearness to the passage into which it is brought, and usually the simple reading of the quotation affords the justification of the writer in using it. But it is not so here. The quotation is harder to deal with than the original text. To find the link that in the writer's mind connects argument and illustration is a far more difficult task than it would be to make out the bare doctrine without any outside help. And these quotations are not a new difficulty. The greatest names, commentators and preachers in the Greek and Latin churches confess and struggle with the exegetical perplexities that try the skill and reverence of their German and English successors. The "fors" and "ands" and "buts" of these chapters grow into a knot of difficulty for the grammarian, and it is oftener cut than unloosed. The marks of quotation, instead of being fingerposts and lights on his path, are often like obstacles that are leaped over or broken through.

The reason of this, partly, is the mystical, rich, deep sense that the Apostle sometimes sees in the Psalms, sometimes put into them : and also partly, I do not doubt, the great change in mental laws and habits in the minds of modern commentators and readers. But the main drift of the Epistle is so clear that the text helps us to interpret its helps and illustrations. Where the quotation does not seem to add strength and clearness to the text, it often gains both from it and thus repays with interest.

These verses have long ranked among passages " hard to be understood "; let us give the more earnest heed to them : earnest thought on a hard text is never without reward. In the first place, then, let us see at what stage we have arrived in the argument.

(1) The aim of the Epistle is to show the authority, the stability, the perfection of the " great salvation " wrought out, and preached, by the Lord. And therefore the writer opens with a discovery of the greatness, the divinity of Him who hath in these last days spoken unto us in the Gospel. Prophets and angels had in former times been messengers of God, and mediators between God and man : but the coming of the Son into human nature has superseded all such mediate and secondary ways of revealing God to man. And not only as the Son of God does this new Mediator still live and work, but He has sat down in our nature, in our interest, on the right hand of the Majesty on High.

Manhood in the Son is set above angel-hood, because He hath, as Son, by inherit-ance a much more excellent name than they.

They did eminent service in the Old Testa-ment church as nearer to God than the sons of men—but in the New, the Son of Man is on the Throne before which they wait and worship, and whence they go forth as ministering spirits in the church of the Son. All this is revealed and established and illustrated in the first chapter.

" Therefore," the second opens, " therefore we ought to give the more earnest heed to the things spoken by the Lord. For if the word spoken by angels was steadfast, how shall we escape if we neglect this greater salvation which has come to us by the Lord of angels, by Him who has all the angels of God worshipping Him. For unto the angels hath God not put in subjection the world to come, but unto man : unto the Man Jesus Christ, unto Him who was made a little lower than the angels for the suffering of death, but is now crowned with glory and honour, having the world to come and all things put under Him."

Such is the connection of the text with what goes before. And now in these four verses before us there are three topics that gather round them the interest of the passage. And these are (1) the Angels, (2) Man, and (3), and as rising out of the second, The Man, *par excellence*, Jesus. Let us examine in the light of Scripture and Christian reason these three topics in order.

And first : the Angels.

The very negative form of the text is a strong affirmation of the existence, and the high dignity and rank, of the angels. They must have had at some time, they must still be capable of having, dominion and power of a very exalted kind when it is felt needful to state and prove that they are not higher than the Son of God. It is surely the very highest tribute to their past service in the world of nature and of grace, when it is said so distinctly that the " world to come " is not put in subjection to them : and when God only did not say to them, " Ye are my sons : sit on my throne : this day have I begotten you."

Man was created, and the Son of Man was born, a little lower than the angels ; but still let it be kept in mind that to Him and not to them the world to come is put into sub-jection. This is the doctrine of the passage. Still their lower place in this text is, I fear, a much higher one than they occupy in the most devout and enlightened, and least sense-bound minds among us. They desire to look into the progress of affairs in the Church, while their service, their very name to us is almost like a vapour of the mind. This Sadducean tone of thought ought not to be allowed in those who are " heirs of salvation " and have faith given to overcome the world and to penetrate into things of the Kingdom of God. It is not in subjection to them : but they had a willing hand in its advent, and they minister continually to its King and His subjects.

The Bible doctrine of the angels may form the stepping-stone to a higher than they. If we believed in and held the Bible doctrine of the world of angels we would oftener pass beyond them to Him who holds their world and ours equally in subjection. It is the same carnal, unchristian state of mind that makes them and their King so unreal, so inoperative on us. It is the same state of mind that so soon leads us to act as if the dead had gone out of existence as well as out of sight, and makes our faith and our feelings so much of the earth, earthy.

Of their nature, Scripture, true to its practical aim, does not say much. They are spirits, partaking in the meantime, at least, more of the nature and likeness of God than man does. But to be spiritual, is not to be incorporeal; that is to say, they, as created, are limited, though not so much subject to time and space and their conditions as we are. Indeed this is the hope of the Resurrection, that we shall then put on spiritual bodies, and in them shall be relieved from the functions that clog and degrade us here, and shall be—it is a distinct promise—"like the angels in heaven." They, like us, were originally created finite, temptable, peccable; they, as a race, had a fall like us; only not being in one Head like man, they fell not all, when some of their number kept not their first estate. But those who fell left their first habitation, each by the act of his own will, and therefore God " hath reserved them in everlasting chains under darkness, unto the judgment of the great day." Hence among them as among men there is a kingdom of sin and death, and a kingdom of grace and life; there is the devil and his angels, and there is the Son of God and the elect angels who minister His will.

Those angels who kept their first estate are constantly represented in Scripture as working beneath and behind the powers of nature. They rule the pestilence that cuts

off the first-born in Egypt; they slay with
disease the murmuring people in the desert;
when David chose to fall into the hand of
God for his chastisement rather than into the
hand of man, the Lord sent a pestilence
under the hand of a destroying angel who
smote seventy thousand men, and was about
to stretch out his hand against Jerusalem
when the Lord said: " It is enough; stay
now thine hand." And when Sennacherib
lay round Jerusalem to besiege it in the days
of Hezekiah, again the angel of the Lord
came forth and smote with sudden death a
hundred and eighty-five thousand men : and
behold ! in the morning they were all dead
corpses. So signal was the hand of God in
it that the King of Assyria immediately
raised the siege and returned to Nineveh.

> For the Angel of Death spread his wings on the
>   blast
> And breathed on the face of the foe as he passed :
> And the eyes of the sleepers waxed deadly and chill
> And their hearts beat and heaved, and for ever were
>   still.

But it is in the scheme of grace that their
ministry is most frequently met with. No
sooner is Abraham called than that gracious

ministry begins : it is the near and trusted
providence of the patriarchs and their house-
holds, and down through the time of the
judges and lawgivers and kings and prophets
of Israel that ministry of angels still waits.
At the incarnation there is a new dispensation of angels; they wait on their King
through all His earthly life, comforting Him
after His temptation, ministering to Him
in His agony, rolling the stone from His
grave, comforting and guiding the disciples,
and after the days of the Spirit have come,
waiting only more secretly and silently in
nature and in grace, ministering in both
spheres to them who shall be the heirs of
salvation.

But these things belong to a spiritual
world, and we are ruled and held down by
our senses, and the material things that
accost us and reign over us through them.
" We look at the things which are seen, and
refuse to look at or hear about the things
which are not seen, though the things which
are seen are temporal, and the things which
are not seen are eternal." And yet did we
but give our minds and the spiritual world
anything like their due, we would learn to

dwell more under the power and in the
solemnising presence of such things. Were
the mind not so clogged and held down, and
its heavenly spring and vigour taken out of
it by sensual labour and sensual pleasures,
there is a touch of divinity about it that
would cause it to ascend and dwell above
the earth. And then, there is so much in
the unseen world to draw the Christian mind
to dwell there. God is there ; His Son, in
our nature, is there ; many of us have most
of our best friends there : those who knew
us best and loved us most, who knew our
secrets and helped us with our burdens—
they are in that world that is not temporal,
that world that is just on the other side of
that quivering vail of flesh that is rending
while I speak. And beyond that vail life is
so much more intense, so much more filled
with feeling, if not with sensation : activity
is unflagging, perception is direct. The dead
are there, but that is the name we in our
ignorance and pride give them : they alone
are truly alive, alive unto God, while we lie
here drenched with sensuality, cribbed and
confined with a body of sin and death. But
while departed saints rest from their labours

in that hidden world, the angels are busy, as
of old, carrying out the will of God in the
spheres of nature and of grace. They are
" ministering spirits set forth to minister for
them who shall be heirs of salvation." " They
are standing on the four corners of the earth,
holding the four winds of the earth, that the
wind should not blow on the earth, nor on
the sea, nor on any tree, till the great angel
having the seal of the living God hath sealed
the servants of our God on their foreheads."
Thus " we are an interest and an occupation,
a spectacle to angels." And as we sink into
the spirit of Holy Scripture we will often
tarry reverently and think about that many-
peopled life, where the spirits of men enter
as they die, where angels live and minister,
where Christ is preparing a place for those
who love Him and look forward to the day
of His reappearing—with His holy angels.

A glance at a good concordance will show
that I have but touched the border of a rich
field of Christian faith and comfort and
reverence in connection with the nature and
ministry of angels.

Still, secondly, it is not to them that God
hath " put in subjection the world to come."

But one in a certain place testifieth, saying : " What is man, that Thou art mindful of him ? or the Son of Man that Thou visitest him ? "

Man is here set over against the angels as originally made a little lower than they, but now crowned with a higher honour and glory. "Thou madest him a little lower than the angels. Thou hast put all things in subjection under his feet." The writer has proved that the Son in our nature is a greater teacher than the angels were : had a greater salvation in commission to reveal : and now he is setting himself to prove that the Son, as Son of Man, is higher in authority than the angels, for, he says : "God hath not put the world to come under them, but under man; it is One raised out of the people who has all things under His feet."

He takes a roundabout way of proving this, as one is tempted to think, but it will repay us to go round the sweep of his thoughts with him. You see he is setting himself to show that " the world to come," the Kingdom of God, in grace here and in glory in heaven, is under man, that it is not under the dominion of angels, nor does God rule it immediately

Himself, but that its responsibilities rest on, and its honour and glory crown, Man—Man as he is found and seen in Jesus, the Son of Man, the Son of God.

And as is his habit, he sees proof and promise of this in the Psalms. And he opens one which, were it not for this quotation and the use made of it, would be among the last to be reckoned as a Messianic psalm. And indeed it is not in the psalm that the Messiah is found, it is rather in that work of God that the psalm celebrates. The psalm sings of man and his glory, but that glory is never found at its best, is never found otherwise than fallen into dishonour and weakness, till it is seen on the New Man, the Lord from Glory. The psalm is Messianic not in the Psalmist's hands, but in the Apostle's.

This quotation and its context are far finer and deeper as read thus than if we were to stuff the Eighth Psalm full of Messianic references, reading in the Epistles between its lines. The force and beauty of the psalm is not in its direct reference to the Messiah—there is none such in it—but in the living, expanding, truly prophetic and Messianic sense that lay in it, because the

Messiah lay in the race whose hymn it was. David did not see Christ in it, nor did he put Him in it. But God had put, was to put, His Son in manhood, and the glory and grace of that nature as sung here as well as its sin and shame gathered round His head when He became the Son of Man.

Look at the Eighth Psalm. It is lyric of a deep, quiet, meditative pious mind. Possibly it may have been suggested to David when keeping his father's few sheep in the wilderness, ere God took him from the sheepfolds, from following the ewes great with young, and brought him to feed Jacob his people, and Israel his inheritance. Looking up at night he sees the splendour of the starry heavens, and thinks of them as all the work of God's fingers, and his devout heart, according to its nature, praises God in a song.

O Lord, our Lord, how excellent is Thy name in all the earth: who hast set Thy glory above the heavens. . . . When I consider the heavens, the work of Thy fingers, the moon and the stars which Thou hast ordained; What is Man—weak, frail, mortal man—that Thou art mindful of him?

And yet, though so humble amid all the glorious work of Thy hands : though made lower than the angels, yet Thou hast crowned him with glory and honour, and hast given him dominion over the work of Thy hands, and put all things under his feet. Much more shall I now say, How excellent, O Lord, is Thy name in all the earth !

David simply, with a devout mind and a pious heart touched with poetic fire, sings of the littleness and the greatness of man as made of the dust of the ground, and yet exalted by the goodness of God to be king of all created things. But when an apostle, writing in these last days after the second Adam has come, and has been crowned with glory and honour, turns to this psalm, he sees a new Man then, and borrows the psalm from natural piety and quotes it in and works it up into Christian doctrine. Man is now so exalted that the glow of Hebrew poetry is not too warm for expressing the actual fact that is accomplished in Christ. Man has his lost lordship and honour restored in Jesus. The crown that had fallen from Adam's head shines again on Jesus ; the sceptre that was a broken reed in the hands of the sons of men, is a sceptre of right and might in the hand of the Son of Man, the Son of God.

Not to angels, but to Jesus, is the spiritual world now made subject—not to angels but to man. This is the plain, direct statement he is seeking to establish. And in going back to the Eighth Psalm the writer goes seemingly off the line of argument, but only that he may strike in on it again in an unexpected way, with new and deeper views of things gathered from what seemed an irrelevant digression. For he has not only exalted Jesus, but taught that His exaltation is the exaltation of man in Him. He sees that this quotation woven into the text will be but a sign and hint and type of how manhood and Godhead, weakness and strength are woven together by the incarnation and exaltation of the Son. The argument seemed needlessly delayed while we were led back to hear David sing of the honours of manhood; but immediately we see Jesus as the Son of Man standing forth on the Apostle's page clothed with all the ideal grace and beauty and majesty of perfect manhood, and the whole sustained by and perpetuated in the person of the Son of God.

Thus man, a Christian man, though originally made a little lower than the angels, has since the days of Jesus been greater in rank than they. He starts a little lower. than they, but since the incarnation is a fact and a power lying and working at the root of human nature, man now starts capable of a growth, and able to face a career greater and wider than that of angels.

For the Son took not on Him the nature of angels. The angels who fell are for ever falling. But He caught hold of us, arrested us, redeemed us, and brought us back to obedience and rest and love and sonship. With an elder Brother such as we have, no praise that we rise above our natural level in the rank of creatures. And with such a Leader and Captain it is no wonder either that the angels stand aside, without a cloud on their faces, or a murmur in their hearts, and accept our promotion and even assist at it. We may well give a more reverent and loving thought to those shining, worshipping, ministering spirits who so kindly take to us and our interests, for His sake who in our nature sits above them. Well may we say with a deeper pathos and humility than David : " What is man that Thou art mindful of him, or the sons of men that Thou hast so visited them ! " And again : " Who am I, O Lord God, and what is mine house that Thou hast brought me hitherto ? . . . And yet this was but a small thing in Thine eyes . . . for Thou hast regarded me according to the estate of a man of high degree ! What is man that Thou art mindful of him ? "

This brings us to the third and last topic in the passage—to Jesus personally.

Three things are said of Him here :

(1) " He was made a little lower than the angels." For He was made like unto His brethren. He who was higher than they : He who had by inheritance a more excellent name than they, was lowered beneath them. He left the seat and home of glory, emptied Himself of His honour and place, passed down through the plane of spiritual life on which they dwelt, left His Father's house and even the courts of it where His servants serve Him, passed out beyond their sphere and entered into a world filled with the colder, darker, grosser, sinful life

of man. So mindful was He of His fallen creature man that He was less mindful of His own life. God made man lower than the angels, but sin had plunged him to an immeasurably lower state : but grace in the Father and the Son reached out after him. For Jesus was made lower than the many ranks of His own creatures, and so made for the suffering of death.

Had He remained what He was He could not have served us by suffered death : had He not remained what He was He could not have recovered it. But He who was Eternal Life came to us that He might endure death, " tasting it for every man." It is quite away from the line of thought to risk any dogmatic position here concerning who they were—all or some—for whom Christ died. For it is not of the Atonement the Apostle is treating, far less the extent of it ; to speak of Christ's death at all is rather the way he takes to share the perfect, complete, out-and-out humanity of the Incarnate Son. It is the Incarnation that he is labouring to set forth in all its rich reference, and deep hold on man, and therefore he carries that thought out into the darkest region of human life, out where death and its awful terrors and sufferings reign. You impoverish this noble passage when you speak of limitations. You degrade it when you drag it into polemics : there is no limitation here but that of race ; He took not on Him the nature of angels, but He took part in the children's flesh and blood, that He might " taste death for every man," and deliver them who through fear of death were all their lifetime subject to bondage. It is not substitution so much that is taught here as that which underlies it—identification, oneness with a sinful race, perfect community with us, with us all, with every man, with our nature : mine and yours, the nature that is sanctified in the Church and corrupted in the world, saved in heaven, lost in hell. This human nature was penetrated through and through with the grace of His Incarnation. Other facts, other relations, other gracious gifts and righteous limitations will rise on and grow from that, but in the interest of all truth we must vindicate the text for the perfect, complete, glorious act of the Incarnation.

The Atonement is indeed in the text, deeply in it, too deeply for raising questions as to its limitations : the Atonement is here but it is as an extension of the Incarnation. It is the incarnate hand of the Son reaching down to the deepest chambers of sin where any son of man might be in fear and chains. He came so as to taste death for every man.

And as it was needful that the Son should take our nature if He was to purge our sin, so it was not expedient that that body He had dwelt in should be left in the grave, and therefore when He had finished His work He took it with Him. He no longer lived apart from our nature, not even from that body He had suffered and died in. He came down lower than the angels that He might enter into it ; and now, when rising to His native seat, He rises in it. He came, the Son ; He lived and died the Christ : He rose and reigns our Lord and Saviour Jesus Christ. And now we see Jesus, who was made a little lower than the angels for the suffering of death, crowned with glory and honour ! or as our author says further on, we " look unto Jesus, who, for the joy that was set before him, endured the cross, despising the shame, and is set down at the right hand of the throne of God." And thus we return and read afresh the great dogmatic passage of Paul : "Let this mind be in you, which was also in Christ Jesus : who, being in the form of God, thought it no robbery to be equal with God : but made himself of no reputation, and took upon him the form of a servant, and was made in the likeness of men : and being found in fashion as a man, he humbled himself, and became obedient unto death, even the death of the cross. Wherefore God hath highly exalted him, and given him a name which is above every name, that at the name of Jesus every knee should bow : and that every tongue should confess that Jesus Christ is Lord, to the glory of God the Father."

Such are the truths set before us in the text concerning the angels, concerning man, and concerning the Man, Jesus Christ.

What remains to be said rises from one word in the text.

The Apostle's remark on the quotation he makes from the Eighth Psalm is : " We see not yet all things put under man. But we do see that come true in the case of one Man, one representative Man, Jesus." The word is the same in the English version : " We see

not all things put under him " (ver. 8, last
clause), "but we see Jesus." The verb is
the same here (ver. 9, first clause), but there
is a most felicitous and suggestive choice of
language in the original Greek.

We see not yet all things put under man.
One cannot open his eyes without seeing
abundant, obtrusive and staring evidence
that man has not yet come into his kingdom.
All creatures, as they are able, are in rebel-
lion against him ; the ground is still cursed
for his sake. There is little glory or honour
to be gathered by the hand of mortal man
in this world. David was a poet, a young
man with a few sheep in the wilderness; and
when he had slain the lion and the bear, delivering the lamb out of his mouth, he was
able to sing : " Thou madest man to have
dominion over the works of thy hands, thou
hast put all things under his feet." The
Apostle quotes it as an ideal pastoral, not
realised in the fields of Israel, but in the
Kingdom of God. It needs, he says, no study
or care to see that all things are not yet
under the dominion of man, but—and the
word is changed from the half-involuntary
impression that one gets just on opening his

eyes—to a word which means earnest looking and directing and fixing of the eye.
We *see* Jesus. By giving earnest and more
earnest heed since first we heard the things
spoken of and by him, by fixing eye and
mind on them so as not to let them slip, we
come to *see* Jesus as all, and more than,
David in his pious lyric said of man at his
best estate. We, who have seen Jesus, see
the meaning and feel the power of His life
and His words, and the words of the prophets
and psalmists concerning Him.

We see Jesus thus not by a heedless glance
or a fitful search, but by looking always for
Him; by searching the Scriptures, and compelling earnest heed to those who search
them for us; by a watchful, eager, delighted
looking for and hanging on Jesus as revealed
and offered in the gospel.

Yes, for the word here points to that kind
of sight, the seat of which is not in the bodily
eye, but in the enlightened understanding,
and in the awakened and loving and brood-
ing tender heart. It is a seeing that has a
strong, intellectual, moral quality in it, and
a strong drawing of desire and delight. It
is a sight that seeks to see more and to

possess all; it is a look that is never filled
with looking; it is the look that when
directed to sinful objects is called, by Jesus
Himself, lust. It is the look that when
directed by the Son to the Father is called
filial love. It is the anxious look of a disciple into the gaze of the risen Master, of
the Twelve on Olivet when He rose and
passed into the heavens, and of those who
watch and pray for His second coming.
These two verbs may be said to divide between them the religion of all who come to
hear the gospel preached. "For if any man
be a hearer of the word and not a doer, he
is like unto a man casually, incidentally
beholding his natural face in a glass: for he
beholdeth himself, and goeth his way, and
straightway forgetteth what manner of man
he was."

But there are happily those also who " with
open face, intently beholding as in a glass the
glory of the Lord, are changed into the same
image even as by the Spirit of the Lord."

" Wherefore he saith : Awake thou that
sleepest and arise from the dead, and Christ
shall give thee light." Let us answer: "Open
thou mine eyes, that I may behold wondrous

things out of thy law!" And of all its wonders this is the sum: to "see Jesus, who was made a little lower than the angels, for the suffering of death, crowned with glory and honour."

V

GABRIEL COMES TO MARY AND TO JOSEPH

And it came to pass, when the priests were come out of the holy place (for all the priests that were present had sanctified themselves, and did not keep their courses;

Also the Levites which were the singers, all of them, even Asaph, Heman, Jeduthun, and their sons and their brethren, arrayed in fine linen, with cymbals and psalteries and harps, stood at the east end of the altar, and with them an hundred and twenty priests sounding with trumpets :)

It came even to pass, when the trumpeters and singers were as one, to make one sound to be heard in praising and thanking the Lord; and when they lifted up their voice with the trumpets and cymbals and instruments of music, and praised the Lord, saying, For he is good; for his mercy endureth for ever: that then the house was filled with a cloud, even the house of the Lord;

So that the priests could not stand to minister by reason of the cloud: for the glory of the Lord had filled the house of God.

GABRIEL COMES TO MARY AND TO JOSEPH

" And in the sixth month the angel Gabriel was sent from God unto a city of Galilee, named Nazareth, to a virgin espoused to a man whose name was Joseph, of the house of David ; and the virgin's name was Mary. And the angel came in unto her, and said, Hail, thou that art highly favoured, the Lord is with thee : blessed art thou among women."—St Luke i. 26-28.

" Now the birth of Jesus Christ was on this wise : When as his mother Mary was espoused to Joseph, before they came together, she was found with child of the Holy Ghost. Then Joseph her husband, being a just man, and not willing to make her a public example, was minded to put her away privily. But while he thought on these things, behold, the angel of the Lord appeared unto him in a dream, saying, Joseph, thou son of David, fear not to take unto thee Mary thy wife : for that which is conceived in her is of the Holy Ghost."—St Matt. i. 18-20.

" Yea, a sword shall pierce through thy own soul also, that the thoughts of many hearts may be revealed."— Luke ii. 35.

[*First given in St George's, 19th November 1883. It caused fierce discussion, and received high praise from Roman Catholic papers. It has never before been printed in full : a shortened form appears in " Bible Characters."*]

THE fulness of time had now come. The time appointed from eternity when God was to send forth His Son made of a woman. This was the most momentous and most gracious hour in the whole history of the human race, for such surely was the incarnation of the eternal and only-begotten Son of God. The Word, who was from the beginning with God, and was God, is now about to be made flesh that henceforth He may dwell among us full of grace and truth. And now, as we draw near to meditate on some of the accompaniments of this mystery, let us have grace that our meditations may be both acceptable unto God and profitable unto ourselves. " Put off thy shoes from off thy feet, for the place whereon thou standest is holy ground."

Six months—speaking of the dispensations of heaven and of the ministries of angels after the manner of men—six months have passed away since Gabriel stood at the right hand of the altar of incense and announced to Zacharias the approaching advent of the Messiah and the immediate birth of John, his forerunner. And now, again, Gabriel, the heavenly baptist, the favoured and fore-running angel of the Annunciation, is sent from God to a city of Galilee, named Nazareth, to a virgin espoused to a man whose name was Joseph, and the virgin's name was Mary.

Gabriel came from God to Mary to announce and open up God's marvellous purposes with her, and at the same time to ask, so to speak, her consent—to ask acceptance of the great destiny that was divinely appointed her and of the great charge that was to be committed to her, as well as to ask her consent and surrender to the heavy cross all this would lay upon her, and to the sharp sword that should soon and again and again pierce through her soul also.

The first and third evangelists tell us all we know of Mary. She was a young woman of Nazareth, who had lately been espoused to a carpenter of that town, named Joseph, and the divine call came to her between her espousal and her marriage. And what a call it was ! And what a prospect it opened up ! And yet, overpowering to her as it then must have been, could she have been told all it contained—could she have known then all that we know now ; could she have seen the end, even as we see it—surely her reason would have reeled on its throne ! As it was, no sooner had she accepted her holy calling, no sooner was she left alone with her own thoughts, than she began to realise something of what had been appointed her, and what she must now prepare herself to pass through. The sharp sword that the aged Simeon afterwards spoke of with such pathos was already whetted and was fast approaching her exposed heart. On a thousand canvases through Christendom we are shown the angel of the Annunciation presenting Mary with a branch of lily, as emblem of her beauty and a seal of her purity, but why has no artist stained the whiteness of the lily with the red blood of a broken heart ? For no sooner had the transfiguring light of the angel's presence faded from her sight than a deep and awful darkness began to fall around Joseph's espoused wife. She already entered the first shadows of that thick cloud which thirty-three years afterwards closed around her forsaken Son. Already the first bitter fruits of that great darkness settled down on Mary's spotless heart and desolated life : settled sometimes, oh so heavy, oh so dark, oh so bitter and hard to bear ! Surely if ever a suffering soul had to seek its righteousness and its refuge and its strength in God alone, it was the soul of the Virgin Mary in the weeks and months that followed the Annunciation !

Blessed among women, as all the time she

was ; unblemished in soul and body as a paschal lamb, yet like that lamb she was set apart to be a sacrifice, and to have a sword thrust through her heart. A blameless, believing woman, though she was, and with seals to her faith, and with assurance and hopes that might well have kept her heart from being too much cast down, yet we may be sure that there were many dark and dreadful seasons when all that she had to support her seemed like a broken reed, and her sorrow seemed greater than she could long bear. If her divine Son Himself had dark and forsaken hours while engaged in His Father's service, much more must His mother have had such hours, with a cloud and a mystery over her young life that had no parallel but His. I just ask you all who are able reverently to go back into that village among the mountains of Galilee and try to realise for yourselves what Mary's feelings and forecasts must often have been. " Blessed among women," the angel had said, and again, " Hail, highly favoured of the Lord," but all that would sometimes seem like mocking words to her, as she saw nothing before her but calumny, repudiation.

an open shame, and, it might be, an outcast's death. And so fearfully and wonderfully are we all made, and so fearful and
wonderful was the way of the Incarnation in
which the Son of God was made in all things
like unto His brethren—that who can tell
how all this bore on Him who was bone of
her bone and flesh of her flesh, to whom
Mary was in all things a mother, as He was
to her in all things most truly a son, for
"hers was the face that unto Christ had
most resemblance."

Oh the mystery of godliness! God manifest in the flesh! Jesus the Son of God and
the Son of Mary: Jesus Christ, the Man of
Sorrows!

Matthew alone tells us Joseph's part in all
this transaction; and as we read the evangelist's account of that time, we see clearly
that Joseph's cross was scarcely, if any, less
heavy than Mary's. His heart was broken
with this terrible catastrophe, but there was
only one course left open to him. Consum-
mate the marriage he could not, but neither
could he consent to make Mary a public, far
less a fatal, example, and there was only left
to him the sad enough step of cancelling the

espousal, putting her away privately. Joseph's
heart, as you can well conceive, was literally
torn in two, for Mary had been the woman
of all women to him ; she had been in his
eyes the lily among thorns. And now to
have to think of her, to have to treat her as
a poisonous weed. The thought of it drove
him mad. " How shall I give thee up,
Ephraim ! How shall I deliver thee, Israel ?
How shall I make thee as Admah ? How
shall I set thee as Zeboim ? Mine heart is
turned within me : my repentings are kindled
together." Oh why is it that whosoever
comes near Jesus Christ has always to drink
such a cup of sorrow ? Truly, truly, they
who are brother, or sister, or mother to him,
must take up their cross daily ! " These are
they who go up through great tribulation."

Amid these circumstances, if thus indeed
they came about, what a journey that must
have been for Mary from Nazareth to Hebron,
and occupied with what thoughts ! As she
journeyed up through the land of Judah
what a glorious past would rise up upon her
devout and well-stored mind, but oh, my
brethren, what an unknown future in that
whole land lay before that lonely maiden !

For she would pass through Jerusalem, and
no doubt she tarried in the city for a night
that she might rest herself and worship, and
restore her heart in the Temple service.   She
may have crossed Olivet as the sun was
setting, she may have knelt at even in
Gethsemane : and she may have turned aside
to look on the city from Calvary.

> O, if all were seen,
> The happiest youth—viewing his progress through
> What perils past, what crosses to ensue—
> Would shut the book, and sit him down and die.

If I am right in my reading of her history,
and if Joseph and Mary had parted before
she left Nazareth in haste, what a cross she
must have carried through all these scenes !
Only two besides God knew the truth about
Mary—an angel in heaven and her own heart
upon earth.   And then it was that Mary
sought the hill country of Judah in such
haste, hoping there to find one who would
receive her word, and understand her case.
As she sped on, Mary must have recalled and
repeated many happy Scriptures, well known
about indeed, but till then little understood.
The husbandmen and vinedressers saw passing them in those days, a Galilean maiden

who seemed to see nothing and hear nothing
as she hastened southwards. Only she would
be overheard, as one communing with her
own heart, saying to herself : " Commit thy
way unto the Lord; trust also in him;
and he shall bring it to pass. And he shall
bring forth thy righteousness as the light,
and thy judgment as the noonday." And
again, " How great is thy goodness which
thou hast laid up for them that fear thee :
which thou hast wrought for them that
trust in thee before the sons of men ! Thou
shalt hide them in the secret of thy presence
from the pride of man : thou shalt keep
them secretly in a pavilion from the strife of
tongues." And such a pavilion Mary sought,
and for a season found, in the remote and
retired household of Zacharias and Elisabeth.

The meeting of Mary and Elisabeth is one
of the most beautiful episodes in Holy Scripture. And it teaches us a happy truth that
we have often had some experience of ourselves—how the crosses and trials of our
lives are relieved, and how faith and hope
and love and joy are revived and increased
as one gracious heart meets with another.
How often, in this very house, have our

lonely, overclouded, disconsolate hearts felt a
new life take possession of them as we came
in and looked around upon the assembled
worshippers, and took up into our lips the
morning psalm and hearkened to what other
men have said to God, and what God said
to them.   When two or three are met in the
name and in the service of God, then His
Holy Spirit is in the midst of them to comfort them and to revive their faith and hope,
their love and joy.   So was it certainly when
these two favoured women met in the house
of Zacharias in the hill country of Judah.
For one thing, it is to that meeting that we
owe the *Magnificat*, the last of Old Testament
psalms, the first of New Testament hymns.
" My soul doth magnify the Lord," said
Mary, " and my spirit hath rejoiced in God
my Saviour." We cannot enter into all
Mary's thoughts as she uttered that melody
any more than she could possibly, in her
day, enter into all our thoughts as we read
and sing it.   Noble melody as her *Magnificat*
is, at the same time to us it draws its deepest
tones from a time that was still to come.
The spirit of Christian prophecy moved her
to utter it, but the noblest and clearest and

fullest prophecy of it is dim and without
glory or blessedness compared with the evangelical fulfilment. A noble psalm as Mary's
Magnificat is, yet the Church sings a nobler
psalm still when she celebrates the praise
of Him who loved her and washed her to
blamelessness and spotlessness in His own
blood.

" And Mary abode with Elisabeth about
three months." She is a happy maiden who
has a mother, or a motherly friend, experienced in the ways of the human heart and
of human life to whom she can tell all her
anxieties. A wise, tender, much experienced
counsellor such as Naomi was to Ruth and
Elisabeth to Mary. Was the Virgin an
orphan that she did not tell it all to her
own mother and find shelter in her bosom till
this calamity was overpast? Or was Mary's
mother a woman such, as sometimes happens
to an anxious maiden, that Mary could have
told it all to any stranger rather than to her?
Be that as it may, Mary found a true mother
in Elisabeth of Hebron. And what happy,
what holy hours the mother and the daughter
spent together sitting under the terebinths
that overhung the dumb priest's secluded

house.   And if at any time during the weeks
and months they spent together their faith
for a moment wavered : if the thing seemed
at any time impossible to them as they looked
at it in the uncongenial and disenchanting
light of daily life, was not Zacharias there
beside them with his sealed lips and his
writing-table, to be as a living witness to
the goodness and severity of God ?   How
Mary and Elisabeth would object and reason,
and rebuke, and confound, and comfort one
another—now laughing like Sarah and now
singing like Hannah—let happy, loving, con-
fiding women tell.

Sweet as it is to linger in Hebron with
Elisabeth and Mary, yet somehow my heart
always draws back to Joseph in desolate and
darkened Nazareth.   "The absent are dear,
just as the dead are perfect."   And Mary's
dear image became to Joseph dearer still
when he could no longer see her face or hear
her voice.   Nazareth was empty to Joseph,
it was worse than empty ; it was a city of
sepulchres to him in which he sought for
death and could not find it.   All the weary
week his bitterness increased, and when, as
his wont was, he went up to the synagogue

on the Sabbath day, that only made him
feel his loneliness and distress the more.
Mary's sweet presence had often made that
holy place still holier to him, and her voice
in the psalms had often been as when an
angel sings. On one of those Sabbaths which
the exiled Virgin was spending with Elisabeth
at Hebron, Joseph went up again to the
sanctuary of God in Nazareth, seeking, as
so many others were no doubt seeking, to
hide his grief with God and to commit his
way to Him. And this, shall I suppose, was
the Scripture appointed to be read in the
synagogue that day :

" Ask thee a sign of the Lord thy God ; ask it either
in the depth, or in the height above. . . . Therefore
the Lord himself shall give you a sign : Behold a virgin
shall conceive, and bear a son, and shall call his name
Immanuel."

Joseph heard Isaiah speak that day as no
man in the house of Israel had ever heard
before. God spake that day in Joseph's
heavy heart. He rose up and found himself at home, a man astonied. When he
laid himself down to sleep that night, his
pillow became a stone under his head. Not
that he was cast out, but that he had cast

out another, and she the best of God's creatures he had ever known! She, perhaps —how shall he utter it even to himself at midnight—she, perhaps, the Virgin Mother of King Messiah. A better mother he could not have. And so, speaking to himself, afraid at what he said to himself, weary with a week's labours, aged with many weeks of uttermost sorrow, Joseph fell asleep. Then a thing was secretly brought to him, and his ear received a little thereof. In thoughts from the visions of the night, when deep sleep falleth on men, then a spirit passed before his face; there was silence, and the sleeper heard a voice saying: " Joseph, thou son of David, fear not to take unto thee Mary, thy wife: for that which is conceived in her is of the Holy Ghost. And she shall bring forth a son, and thou shalt call his name Jesus: for he shall save his people from their sins."

Gabriel had come in the name of God, to reassure the despairing heart of the bridegroom, to demand of him the consummation of the broken-off marriage, and to announce the Incarnation of the Son of God; he had even told Joseph the Heaven-given name of the divine Child who was thus committed to his fatherly care.

Did Joseph arise before daybreak on the first day of the week and set out for Hebron to bring his outcast home ? There is room to believe that he did. If he did, I think the two angel-chastened men had their own counsels together, even as the two women had. And as Joseph talked with Zacharias through his writing-table, he must often have felt that dumbness, and even death itself, would have been but a too light punishment for unbelief like his. But all this, and all that had been passed through since Gabriel came to Zacharias at the altar; all that the four favoured ones had passed through would only make the re-betrothal of Joseph and Mary that took place at Hebron the sweeter and holier : with the still dumb priest to act the part of a father, and with aged Elisabeth acting more than the part of a mother. The unbelief of Zacharias and his consequent infirmity have, no doubt, bereft us of a doxology over Joseph and Mary that would worthily have stood on the evangelist's page beside Mary's *Magnificat* and his own *Benedictus*.

And now to sum up. There are many things in Mary's character and example that cannot escape the attention of every reader of her marvellous history : many things that cannot surely miss imitation in many of her sisters here. But there is one thing not found in every one of her age and sex that I must ask all women's attention to, and that is her early thoughtfulness, her singular sobriety and seriousness of mind. I, for my part, do not know the virtue that woman ever had, that I could safely deny to Mary. The divine congruity and moral fitness of things all compel me to believe that all that could well be received and attained and possessed by any woman would, almost of necessity, be granted beforehand to her who was so miraculously to bear, and so intimately to nurture, and instruct, and guide, and be-friend, and in all things be an example to the holy child Jesus. What a revealing light Mary's motherhood sheds back upon her girlhood and youth ! What she must have been who was designated and chosen to be the mother of Jesus Christ !

My brothers, you must join with me in giving Mary her due : her due promised her

by the announcing angel. You must not
cherish a grudge at Mary because some have
given her more than her due. There is no
fear of any of you thinking too much—either
of Mary's maidenly virtues or of her motherly
duties and experiences. But the Holy Ghost
in guiding the researches of Luke and co-
operating with that evangelist in the composition of his Gospel seems to me specially
to signalise the thoughtfulness and the depth
and the placidity of Mary's maidenly mind.
Thus at the salutation of the angel she did
not swoon, or cry out: she did not rush
either into terror, on the one hand, or transport on the other. But like a wise and a
believing woman, the evangelist tells us
that she cast in her mind what manner of
salutation this should be. And later on,
when all were wondering at the accounts of
the shepherds, it is quietly and suggestively
added: "But Mary kept all these things
and pondered them in her heart." And yet
again, after another twelve years have passed
over her, we still find the evangelist signalis-
ing this as the great distinguishing feature
in her saintly character: "They understood
not the saying which Jesus spake unto them.

But his mother kept all these sayings in her heart." Where thoughtfulness like this is found in man or woman, any virtue, any grace, may be looked for under its shelter. Any amount and any quality of service may be expected of that youth or maiden who exhibits Mary's depth, reasoning and thoughtfulness of mind.

But again, if we are to apply the principle in Mary's case, and with all our jealousy of her I do not see how we can make an exception—the principle, " according to your faith so be it unto you "—then it seems to me Mary must wear the crown as the mother of all who believe in her Son. If Abraham's faith made him their father, then surely Mary's faith entitles her to be called their mother. If the converse of Christ's words hold true—His words to the effect that no mighty works are done where there is unbelief—if, I say, it is conversely true that where there has been a mighty work done there must have been a corresponding faith —then I leave it to you to say what manner and what measure of faith Mary's must have been. If this was the mightiest work ever wrought by God among the children of men

—as all subsequent Scripture shows it to
have been—and if Mary's faith entered into,
it at all—then, I repeat, how great her faith
must have been! Elisabeth saw how great
it was. She perceived the unparalleled
nature of the grace that had come to Mary;
she had humility enough to acknowledge it
and to utter it in her salutation : " Blessed
art thou among women, and blessed is the
fruit of thy womb. . . . And blessed is she
that believed, for there shall be a perform-
ance of those things which were told her from
the Lord."

Yes, Mary received the angel's astounding
message with a beautiful simplicity and a
noble trust. She neither manifested the
levity and mocking incredulity of Sarah,
nor the downright unbelief of Zacharias.
" Blessed is she that believed," said Elisabeth, no doubt with some allusion to her
helpless husband sitting beside her.

" Blessed," on one occasion afterwards
cried a nameless woman, a nameless but
a true woman, as her speech betrayeth :
" Blessed is the womb that bare thee, and
the paps which thou hast sucked." But He
said : " Yea, rather, blessed are they that

hear the word of God and keep it." And again, " Whosoever shall do the will of my Father which is in heaven, the same is my brother, and sister, and mother." Yes, my brethren, none of you will believe it so as to possess the blessedness of it; but to hear God's word and to keep it, to do the will of God, is more than to have been the highly favoured woman of whose flesh He was made, and who bore Him, and gave Him unto the world. And thus we may say that every ambassador of Christ is among you from God as a better Gabriel, and that every gospel message is a new Annunciation, and every believer's Redemption Song a nobler *Magnificat.*

" Blessed is the womb that bore thee ! " " Yea, rather, blessed are they that hear the word of God and keep it."

VI

THE ANGEL OF THE AGONY

How oft do they their sylvan bowers leave
To succour us that succour want.

SPENSER'S *Faery Queene*

THE ANGEL OF THE AGONY

" And he came out, and went, as he was wont, to the
Mount of Olives; and his disciples also followed him.
And when he was at the place, he said unto them, Pray
that ye enter not into temptation. And he was withdrawn
from them about a stone's cast, and kneeled down, and
prayed, saying, Father, if thou be willing, remove this
cup from me : nevertheless not my will, but thine, be done.
And there appeared an angel unto him from heaven,
strengthening him. And being in an agony he prayed
more earnestly : and his sweat was as it were great drops
of blood falling down to the ground. And when he rose
up from prayer, and was come to his disciples, he found
them sleeping for sorrow, and said unto them, Why sleep
ye ? rise and pray, lest ye enter into temptation."—LUKE
xxii. 39-46.

DURING the Passover week Jerusalem could
not half contain the crowds of worshippers
that flocked up to the feast from all corners
of the land. It was enough if the men of
Galilee could as much as get their foot within
the sacred gate, and have their lamb slain
before the sacred altar. The supper itself
could be eaten in any hired room, or in any
of the ten thousand tents that filled the
surrounding valleys : the lately relaxed law
allowed that the paschal lamb could even be

carried out as far as Bethany and eaten there.
There was nothing strange, therefore, in our
Lord and His disciples first celebrating the
feast in the Upper Room, and then passing
out of the city gates to spend what remained
of the sacred night among the olive trees
of Gethsemane. Our Lord had lodged for
several nights previously in this same Gethsemane. He had supped and slept at Bethany
last Sabbath night; but since then this is
the condensed diary of His occupations and
whereabouts: " In the daytime He was
teaching in the temple : and at night He
went out and abode in the mount that is
called the Mount of Olives." And thus we
go on to read quite naturally that " when
He and His disciples had sung an hymn after
supper they went out to the Mount of Olives."
The spot on the Mount of Olives toward
which our Lord directed His feet was a
familiar spot to Him and to all His disciples.
It was a garden, enclosed and private, but it
was put at His entire disposal by the pro-
prietor, who seems to have been a secret
disciple. The gate of this garden was always
open to our Lord. Inside its fence He had
found retirement and rest from the fatigues

of the day during all the past week; and
hither He again came that solemn Thursday
night as soon as He had eaten the Passover
with His disciples in the Upper Room. It
was now midnight, or very near it. The
paschal moon was high in heaven, and the
night was cold, but the city was all astir like
noonday when Jesus went over the brook
Kedron and entered Gethsemane with His
eleven disciples.

No sooner had the gate of Gethsemane
closed behind them than their Master drew
toward Himself Peter and the two sons of
Zebedee, and led them away deeper into the
darkness of the garden, saying to the other
eight, " Sit ye here while I go yonder and
pray." And it was when He was left alone
with His three chosen disciples that He began
to enter into His agony. Almost the last
words He had spoken to them had been
these : " In the world ye shall have tribulation, but be of good cheer : I have overcome the world." But now, all of a sudden,
it seemed as if He Himself was wholly
overcome of sorrow : He seemed suddenly
crushed to the very earth with it. The
three terrified disciples had never seen any

sorrow like this before. They had often seen
their Master sad, they had often seen Him
in deep trouble, they had sometimes seen
Him in tears ; but they had never seen Him
so daunted, so overwhelmed, and so bowed to
the earth as He suddenly became among the
olive trees of Gethsemane. They saw nothing in the garden to account for this so sudden
change in their Master. The language they
used to describe that moment, in describing
it afterwards, shows us how utterly un-
precedented their Master's state of mind at
that moment was ; and how vain were all
their attempts to tell the others, who had
not seen it, the sadness of Gethsemane. " He
began to be sorrowful and very heavy," says
one. " He began to be sore amazed and
very heavy," says another. " And being in
an agony," says a third, " His sweat was as
it were great drops of blood falling to the
ground." What they here write might also
be interpreted thus : " He seemed to be on
the brink of despair. . . . He was like a man
astonied, and beside Himself, with fear and
sorrow. . . . He seemed to us as if He were
in His death-agony."

" He began to be sorrowful." There is

something very mysterious, and not easily to
be understood, in this word " He began."
It points to something in this sorrow utterly
unlike any other sorrow. For our Lord
enters, as it would seem, into His great
sorrow of His own accord. He prepares
Himself for it. He disposes of His disciples
with a view to it. He has long looked
forward to this night of sorrow : and now
that it has come He deliberately lays Himself out to meet it. For this hour He had
been born ; for this hour He had come into
this world ; against this hour John, His
forerunner, had hailed Him as the " Lamb
of God "; nay, for this hour He had been
the Lamb slain from before the foundation
of the world. This is the supreme hour of
His earthly life. He now takes upon Himself the awful burden that to-morrow He will
take away upon the tree. For it was just
when He had taken Peter and James and
John apart ; it was just at that fore-ordained
and supreme moment that God laid on
Him the iniquity of us all ; and put into
His hand the terrible cup of our trans-
gressions. And thus it is that it is said He
began to be sorrowful. He had been the

Man of Sorrows from His youth up : " Himself had taken our infirmities and had borne our sicknesses "; but in all that He had only been preparing Himself for this hour. All His past suffering had been but stepping-stones and foretastes to this, and therefore all His past of pain and sorrow was swallowed up in the pain and sorrow of Gethsemane.

" He began to be sore amazed," says Mark, with all his wonted point and vividness. " He began to be sore amazed." We read that word over and over again. We stop and stand still at that startling word. " He began to be sore amazed." We tremble before His sore amazement more than before all His other agony. And well we may. For our redemption seems to be costing our Redeemer more than He had calculated on. " All this ! " He seems to say in His amazement. " All this : and all this ! " He is staggered and struck down thus early with a horror He had not reckoned upon. More is to be demanded of Him for our forgiveness than He had undertaken, or, at least, had wholly realised. " Who knoweth the power of Thine anger ? " we seem to hear Him say. " Even according to Thy fear, so is Thy wrath."

The amazement that fell on our Lord in Gethsemane was an amazement we are totally unable to understand or to conceive. For we have never felt it, or anything like it, and never, in this world, will. We have felt, and have expressed amazement at many things, but we have never felt any true amazement at that which so amazed our Lord in the garden. We are never truly or adequately amazed at sin. Sin dwells in us. It has been inherited by us and we have ourselves committed it in many forms. Our own sin lies heavy upon us, and other men's sins have been laid upon us. But no man is at all amazed at it, or in genuine sorrow of soul on account of it, or is any the less alive, not to say near death, because of it. To tell the truth, we wonder what all that agony is about. If it were any one else but Jesus Christ we would take him and rebuke him for it. We have been exceeding sorrowful and very heavy and nigh unto death about other things, but never about sin. No! He trod His winepress alone in His amazement at sin, as well as in all the other elements of His atoning agony.

He had often, from His youth up, been

amazed at sinners, at their falls, at their madness, at their unutterably evil and miserable lot; and especially at their ignorance of it, contentment with it, and determination not to be delivered out of it. He had wondered at their unbelief when He preached of sin and salvation to them. He had looked down with shame and horror into human hearts; with anger and with amazement into the hearts of His own disciples; and had steadfastly set His face to pay any demanded price to set them free from sin. Sin and sinners were not a new study to Jesus Christ in the Garden of Gethsemane, but He learned a new knowledge about sin among its dark olive trees that Passover night. For, to His sore amazement and unspeakable horror, He suddenly found Himself made sin. To His utter prostration of soul, His Father at that awful moment laid on Him the iniquity of us all. Though He had done no sin, though He had kept Himself, though the Accuser of mankind had nothing in Him: yet, here in some utterly amazing way, He is made sin. He hated sin as He hated nothing else. He loathed sin as He loathed nothing else. He never

in thought or in word or in deed admitted
the hell-born thing into Himself, and yet,
here it all is laid upon Him, clinging to Him;
clinging to Him and claiming Him for its
own, filling His whole soul with its shame
and its guilt and horror. " Let this cup
pass ! " He cried out in His amazement and
His agony. " If it be possible, let this cup
pass ! " He had hoped to suffer for sin in
silence. " As a Lamb brought to the slaughter
is dumb "—this had been His vow, intention,
and expectation. But in His utter amazement and extreme agony He forgot all that,
for this is a cup of a kind it had not entered
into His thought to conceive.

At the same time, bitter beyond all His
anticipations and foretastes as the cup turned
out to be, and nigh as His soul was unto
death even in lifting it up to drink it, yet,
even in His uttermost extremity He never
for a moment forgot who He was, and what
His errand was on this earth, and especially
what His errand was that midnight in Gethsemane. More bitter His cup could not
possibly be, nor more utter His amazement
at the nature of its ingredients ; but had it
been a thousand times more bitter and His

amazement at it a thousand times more overpowering—yet it would not all have shaken the faith or turned the final purpose of our Blessed Redeemer. " Abba, Father," He said, " all things are possible unto Thee : take away this cup from Me : nevertheless, not what I will, but what Thou wilt." Not more than an hour had elapsed since the same lips had said : " Father, I will that they whom Thou hast given Me be with Me where I am ; that they may behold My glory." But when He said that He was for the moment out of the body, and was sat down for a short season at God's right hand. That was a moment of transfiguration granted Him to strengthen Him for this hour in the garden, and for to-morrow's three hours upon the tree. The intercessory prayer was offered by our Heavenly Priest in the Holy of Holies, and before the Mercy Seat ; the petition, " if it be possible," was the one extorted cry of the Lamb of God as He was being suddenly bound to the horns of the altar. " If it be possible," He said, knowing full well all the time that it was not possible. No, it was not possible, and even if it had been possible He would not have accepted

the offered deliverance. But many things
combined to make such a deliverance impossible. Impossibility upon impossibility made
it impossible. The things that belonged to
our redemption had gone too far. The heart
of God was too deeply set upon it. The
honour of God was too deeply committed
to it. The Son of God had travelled too
far toward it; His best joy and sweetest
blessedness were now too dependent on it.
Too many saints had been let fall asleep in
the sure hope of it, and too many, yet unborn,
were eternally predestinated to partake of it.
Holy Scripture was too full of it, and its promises had been published too widely in the
faith of it. All this, and far more than all
this, made it altogether impossible that the
cup shall pass from Jesus Christ in the
garden. The indissoluble knot that knits
Godhead and manhood together for ever in
our Redeemer shall be strained to its utmost
tension : God the Son shall agonise into a
sweat of blood, nay, He shall die to-morrow
an Outcast on the accursed tree : all that is
possible, and all that shall take place, but
it is not possible surely that one drop shall
be spilt or left undrunk of that bitter

cup; it is not possible that one believing sinner shall be lost, or that so much as one hair of his head shall perish. Three times our Saviour tried this impossible way in His amazement and agony, and three times He returned of His own accord to take the cup. Three times He prayed on His knees and on His face to His Almighty Father, and three times He took away this better answer: " My Grace is sufficient for Thee: for My strength is made perfect in weakness."

Who the Angel of the Agony was, and in what way he strengthened our Lord that midnight, our evangelist does not tell us. It was not bodily strength He needed so much as spiritual. He will need bodily support also before He finishes His work on Calvary to-morrow; but it is His soul that is exceeding sorrowful even unto death to-night. Whoever the angel was, and in whatever form he may have appeared, the true strength he was commissioned to carry to the Man of Sorrows was spiritual strength. That is to say, it was the Holy Ghost who somehow descended into the sinking soul of our Saviour and somehow refreshed and

revived and strengthened Him. It may have
been by recalling some of the more magnificent Messianic passages of the Old Testament
to His mind, and impressing them with the
Holy Spirit's utmost power on our Saviour's
heart. It may have been by some extra-
ordinarily intimate and powerful sealing of
our Lord's sinking soul with uttermost assurance of ultimate victory and everlasting
acceptance of Himself and His work in
heaven. He had been strengthened in that
way at the Jordan and again on the Mount
of Transfiguration, and it may well have
been that at this terrible crisis in the history
of heaven and earth, when the Lord of both
was sinking under our sins, that the Holy
Ghost descended, as never before nor since,
to fill the fainting soul of our Saviour with
the full strength of God. No doubt the best,
because a divinely designed comment on
our present passage is that in the Epistle to
the Hebrews : " Jesus, the Author and
Finisher of our Faith, for the joy that was
set before Him, endured the Cross, despising
the shame." The Holy Ghost may have so
set our Lord's coming joy before Him in
Gethsemane as with it to lighten up its

gross darkness, and sweeten His death-bitter
cup.

But, let this be attended to and let it not
escape you, that it was after His first prayer
was offered and answered; it was after the
angel from heaven had come and strengthened
Him and had departed; it was after all that
that our Lord entered into His real agony.
It is after the account of the angel that we
go on to read that, " being in an agony, He
prayed more earnestly: and His sweat was
as it were great drops of blood falling down
to the ground." The angel was sent to
strengthen our Lord in answer to His prayer
that the cup might pass from Him. The
cup was not to pass, but He was strengthened
to take it up. And then it was that with
the cup in His hand, so to speak, He went
away alone the second time and " prayed
more earnestly," prayed in an " agony " of
prayer and said: " O my Father, if this cup
may not pass from me except I drink it,
Thy will be done." His agonising prayer
now was not that the cup might pass from
Him, but rather that He might be made able
to drink it. If I may say so, His first prayer
was for Himself, for His own deliverance

from the cup and from the Cross; but His second and much more earnest prayer was for us, for us and for His Father, for His Father's will and for our salvation. His great agony was not because He must drink the cup, but, rather, lest He should fail in drinking it. In His agony and amid His bloody sweat, He offered up prayers and supplications with strong crying and tears, and was heard in that He feared. Now, the thing He so feared could not be the cup, because He was not heard in His prayer concerning it, but what He so feared as to be in an agony of prayer on account of it, was lest He should not be found able to drink the cup and thus finish His work. "His spirit was willing, but His flesh was weak." He held the cup in His willing hand, but He feared lest He should fail in fully drinking it, and He feared, and well He might, the terrible shock and strain of the atonement. The thought of failure in that threw Him into an agony, and in His agony a bloody sweat broke out all over His body. And no wonder, for as He took into His hand the terrible cup, heaven and hell both lay open before Him. Heaven hung

silent over Him, its very Hallelujahs hushed
till He should finish His work. And hell
stood open beneath Him to swallow quick
all His Father's elect if He failed in that He
now feared. What words He took to His
Father in His agony we are not told, but no
doubt they were well-known words the Holy
Ghost had prepared for Him in Holy Scripture. We know what psalms were in His
heart and on His lips when He hung on the
Cross, and it may well have been that He
took such psalms as this to the Throne of
Grace in His agony. Had the disciples not
been sleeping for sorrow they might have
heard such supplications as these rising to
heaven from among the dark olives of
Gethsemane : " Save me, O God, for the
waters are come in unto my soul. I sink
in deep mire, where there is no standing : I
am come into deep waters where the floods
overflow me. . . . Deliver me out of the
mire, and let me not sink . . . let not the
waterflood overflow me, let not the pit shut
his mouth upon me. . . . Be not Thou far
from me, O Lord, O my strength, make
haste to help me."

We read and we speak of " agonies " and

we sometimes endure them ourselves. But this world, so full of agony from the beginning, never saw an agony like the agony of Gethsemane. Not Adam's great agony when he was driven out of Eden, fallen from righteousness, accursed, naked and ashamed. Not Noah's agony, when he awoke from his wine and saw what his younger son had done unto him. Not Esau's agony, when he vainly sought a place of repentance. Not Moses', when he was shut out of Canaan. Not David's, when Nathan said to him, "Thou art the man," or when his moisture was turned into the drought of summer. Not Peter's, when he wept bitterly, nor Paul's in his keen and incurable wretchedness on account of his sin. All those agonies entered into Christ's agony, composed it, contributed to it; for the Lord had laid on Him the iniquity of us all. But blessed be the God and Father of our Lord Jesus Christ, He was heard in that He feared. For He agonisingly asked for sufficient strength, and sufficient strength was sent to Him. He called with strong crying and tears, and His Father hearkened and heard. And now, out of that agony, through that cup and through

His coming Cross, we have received the atonement.

Only, my brethren, have we ? Have we in very truth and in very deed received the atonement ? Have we read it in the Word of God ? Have we thence received it into our Creed ? Have we thence received it into our conscience ? Have we so received it ? And have we so kept it ? If so, if by the great grace of God to us it is so, then we can say with the great Apostle of the atonement, " The sting of death is sin, and the strength of sin is the law. But thanks be to God who giveth us the victory through our Lord Jesus Christ." Take away the atonement and you leave us of all men most miserable. For seven times every day, nay, seventy times seven the remorses of our conscience and the corruptions of our heart compel us to Gethsemane. Shut that gate against us, silence that garden of its awful agony, and you make us fugitives and vagabonds on the earth, and every one that findeth us shall slay us. Out of Gethsemane we have no place on this earth to lay our guilty head. An Example ? A Teacher ? A Prophet come from God ? A King ? Yes,

surely. All that and always all that. For
who but Jesus Christ shall ever be to us
Example, Teacher, Prophet or King ? But
what of my sin ? Where is my sin and my
guilt ? Where is my lifetime of sin, if Christ
is not for it a Sacrifice ? Evacuate your
Gospel of the atonement, and it ceases to be
a Gospel to me. Take Christ down off the
accursed tree, and you have taken away my
Lord. Take His blood out of your fountain,
and where will you wash me clean ? Remove
the scandal of His Cross from before the
Mercy Seat and you shut my mouth in the
middle of my confession and supplication,
and send me forth to seek a place of repentance with despairing tears. Soften the Cross
out of my Creed and you effectually shut my
mouth as an accuser of sinners and as an
ambassador to them : nor can I any more
truly comfort the people of God.

> When I survey the wondrous Cross
> On which the Prince of Glory died,
> My richest gain I count but loss,
> And pour contempt on all my pride.
>
> See from His head, His hands, His feet,
> Sorrow and love flow mingled down ;
> Did ere such love and sorrow meet,
> Or thorns compose so rich a crown ?

VII

THE ANGEL OF THE CHURCH OF EPHESUS

THE ANGEL OF THE CHURCH OF EPHESUS

"Unto the angel of the church of Ephesus write; These things saith he that holdeth the seven stars in his right hand, who walketh in the midst of the seven golden candlesticks. I know thy works, and thy labour, and thy patience, and how thou canst not bear them which are evil: and thou hast tried them which say they are apostles, and are not, and hast found them liars: and hast borne, and hast patience, and for my name's sake hast laboured, and hast not fainted. Nevertheless, I have somewhat against thee, because thou hast left thy first love. Remember therefore from whence thou art fallen, and repent, and do the first works; or else I will come unto thee quickly, and will remove thy candlestick out of his place, except thou repent. But this thou hast, that thou hatest the deeds of the Nicolaitanes, which I also hate. He that hath an ear, let him hear what the Spirit saith unto the churches; To him that overcometh will I give to eat of the tree of life, which is in the midst of the paradise of God."—REVELATION ii. 1-7.

You are not to think of an angel with six wings. This is neither a Michael nor a Gabriel. I cannot give you this man's name, but you may safely take it that he was simply one of the oldest of the office-bearers of Ephesus. No, he was no angel. He was just a chosen and faithful elder who had begun by being a deacon and who had purchased to himself a good degree, like any one of yourselves. Only, by reason of his great age and his spotless character and his outstanding services, he had by this time risen till he was now at the head of what we would call the kirk-session of Ephesus. By universal acclamation he was now the "president of their company and the moderator of their actions," as Dr John Rainoldes has it. This angel, so to call him, had grown grey in his eldership, and he was beginning to feel that the day would not now be very far distant when he would be able to lay down his office for ever. At the same time it looked to him but like yesterday when he had heard the prince of the apostles saying to him those never-to-be-forgotten words: "Take heed to thyself, and all the flock over which the Holy Ghost hath made thee an overseer, to feed the Church of God, which He hath purchased with His own blood." And, with many mistakes, and with many shortcomings, this ruling and teaching elder of Ephesus had not been wholly unmindful of his ordination vows. In short, this so-called angel of the Church of Ephesus was no more an actual angel than I am. A real angel is an angel. And we cannot attain to a real angel's nature, or to his office, so as to describe such an angel aright. But we understand this Ephesus elder's nature and office quite well. We see his very same office every day among ourselves. For his office was just to feed the flock of God, as Paul has it. And again, as James has it, his office was just to visit the widows and orphans of Ephesus in their affliction, and to keep himself unspotted from the world of Ephesus. And he who has been elected of God to such an office as that in Ephesus, or in Edinburgh, or anywhere else, has no need to envy the most shining angel in all the seven heavens. For the most far-shining angel in the seventh heaven itself desires to look down into the pulpit and the pastorate of the humblest and obscurest minister in the Church of Christ. And that because he knows quite well that there is nothing for him to do in the whole of heaven for one moment to be compared with the daily round on this earth of a minister, or an elder, or a deacon, or a collector, or a Sabbath school teacher.

Now there is nothing so sweet, either among angels or among men, as to be appreciated and praised. To be appreciated and praised is the wine that maketh glad the heart of God and man. And the heart of the old minister of Ephesus was made so glad when he began to read this Epistle that he almost died with delight. And then as His all-seeing and all-rewarding way always is, His Lord descended to instances and particulars in His appreciation and praise of His servant. " I know thy works. I chose thee. I gave thee all thy talents. I elected thee to thy charge in Ephesus. I ordained thee to that charge, and My right hand hath held thee up in it. Thou hast never been out of My mind or out of My eye or out of My hand for a moment. I have seen all thy work as thou wentest about doing it for Me. It is all written before Me in My book. All thy tears also are in My bottle."

We have an old-fashioned English word that exactly sets forth what our Lord says next to the angel of Ephesus. " I know all thy painfulness also," He says. It is a most excellent expression for our Master's purpose. No other language has produced so many painful ministers as the English language, and no other language can so well describe them. For just what does this painfulness mean ? It means all that is left behind for us to fill up of His own painful sufferings. It means all that tribulation through which every true minister of His goes up. It means cutting off now a right hand and plucking out now a right eye. It means taking up some ministerial cross every day. It means drinking every day the cup of the sinfulness of sin. It means to me old Thomas Shepard more than any other minister I know. " Labour," as our bloodless version has it, is a far too dry, a far too wooden, and a far too tearless, word for our Lord to employ toward such servants of His. Depend upon it, He will not content Himself with saying " labour " only. He will select and will distinguish on that day. And to all who among ourselves have preached and prayed and have examined themselves in and after their preaching and praying, as it would seem that this angel at one time did, and as Thomas Shepard always did, their Master will signalize and appreciate and praise their " painfulness " in their own so expressive old English, and they will appreciate and appropriate His so suitable word and will appreciate and praise Him back for it.

VIII

FULNESS OF JOY

Ye watchers and ye holy ones,
Bright Seraphs, Cherubim, and Thrones,
Raise the glad strain, Alleluia !
Cry out Dominions, Princedoms, Powers,
Virtues, Archangels, Angels' choirs,
Alleluia !

O higher than the Cherubim,
More glorious than the Seraphim,
Lead their praises, Alleluia !
Thou Bearer of the eternal Word,
Most gracious, magnify the Lord,
Alleluia !

FULNESS OF JOY

" His presence is Salvation."—PSALM xlii. 5 (Margin).
" In thy presence is fulness of joy."—PSALM xvi. 11.

[*First given in St George's, Edinburgh, 23rd December* 1906.]

To be in any man's presence is to be near
him.   It is to be in the same house with him.
It is to be in the same room with him.   It
is to see him and to hear him.   And it is
that he should see and hear us.   But God's
presence is not like that.   God's presence is
not to be sought for in any one time, or
in any place, like a man's presence.   God
Almighty does not dwell within the limits of
time and space as He has made man to dwell.
" God is a Spirit, infinite, eternal and un-
changeable."   He inhabiteth eternity.   He
only hath immortality.   He dwelleth in the
light which no man can approach unto.   No
man hath seen God at any time.   The palace
of the King of Kings is not built of ivory and
cedar wood and precious stones.   His royal
seat has been built from everlasting, and it

has been built of wisdom and power, and holiness and justice, and goodness and truth. And, if He has a presence-chamber anywhere at all, let Him describe His presence-chamber to us Himself. "For thus saith the High and lofty One that inhabiteth eternity, whose name is Holy : I dwell in the high and holy place, with him also that is of a contrite and humble spirit, to revive the spirit of the humble and to revive the heart of the contrite ones." And again, "The heaven is my throne and the earth is my footstool. For all those things hath mine hand made, saith the Lord. But to this man will I look, even to him that is poor and of a contrite spirit, and trembleth at my word." There is no possibility of mistaking that. We shall never, to all eternity, fully understand the metaphysical presence of God, but even now and here we shall all enjoy His gracious presence and the light of His countenance, so far as we are of a humble and a contrite heart.

At the same time, absolutely impossible as it is for us at all to comprehend the bottomless mystery of the divine Omnipresence, at the same time we cannot employ our minds better than by dazzling them and staggering them with such thoughts as these : *Deus ubique est : et totus ubique est.* That is to say, God is everywhere, and He is wholly everywhere. Just to take that first principle of the Divine Nature and to dwell upon it and to call it up continually in our minds, and to enter, as far as may be, into it, and to feed our souls upon it, and to take a majestic joy out of it—to what more blessed use can we put our best minds and all that is within us. And again, to take this : that in God all things live and move, and have their being : absolutely all things—from a grain of sand up to a solar system, and from a coral insect up to an archangel. Oh, my brethren, meditate much on these things. And give yourselves to the worship, and the obedience, and the love and the enjoyment of Him of whom all these things are true—and of whom the half has not been told.

" When I was a child, I thought as a child." But the " presence of God " is not " above " us in a geometrical or in an astronomical sense, as I once thought it was. If the presence of God is " above " us at all, it is above us in an intellectual and a spiritual sense.

God's presence-chamber is not entered by
the way of Orion and the Pleiades, but by the
way of a broken and a contrite heart. It is
by the lowly way of repentance, and faith,
and prayer, and love, and holiness, and
the strait gate. What ! Know ye not that
the Kingdom of God is within you ? The
City of the great King, with all its gates of
one pearl, and all its streets of gold, and all
its walls of jasper—all, all is in the regenerate
and holy hearts of God's people. You must
all have read John Bunyan's *Holy War*, a
piece of sanctified genius only second to the
Pilgrim's Progress itself. And you cannot
have forgotten the city of *Mansoul*, with its
gates, and its walls, and its streets, and the
palace of Immanuel in the centre of the city.
" This is my seat for ever," said the King's
Son. " Here will I dwell, for I have desired
it."

There is a little finger-length of a book
entitled *Brother Lawrence on the Practice
of the Presence of God*. The little book is in
its fiftieth thousand, and it is a good sign
of things that it is so. You could get it
bound in French morocco for half-a-crown,
suitable for a Christmas present, and in

paper covers for sixpence. And if your friend were to read it—and it is a very small book —and were to follow its precepts, and these are most winningly set forward, it would be the best laid-out half-crown that ever you or he transacted all your days. " If I were a preacher," says the brother in one place, " I should above all other things preach the practice of the presence of God." Yes, and if I enjoyed the presence of God like that eminent saint, I would preach it like him. But as Peter Bohler said to John Wesley: " Preach faith till you get it and then preach it because you have got it." So, I have no doubt what Brother Lawrence would say to me about preaching this presence of God. Let me preach it then, and let you hear it till we both get it. And since we can only get it by preaching and practising it, let us proceed to learn one or two lessons this morning in that holiest and most blessed of all practices.

(1) And to begin with, let us " practise the presence of God " by a firm faith in God, and a firm faith in His presence. God and His presence will come to be almost an object of sense to us, almost a matter of sight and touch to us, if we sufficiently practise it.

But for a long time it must be a practice of
pure faith. You do not need faith to practise
the presence of any of your fellow-creatures.
You can see them. You can touch them
with your hands any day you choose. But
not God. No man with his eyes hath
seen God at any time. And thus it is that
" he that cometh to God must believe that
He is." His faith must be, as it were, the
" substance " of his God to him. His faith
must be to him the " evidence " of his God's
very existence to him, as the Apostle so nobly
and so boldly has it—so much so, that faith,
as it were, creates her God and sustains his
ideal. God lives, and moves, and has His
being, so to say, in His people's faith in Him.
He is: He eternally and absolutely is, apart
altogether from them and from their faith in
Him. But it is their faith in Him that makes
Him to be for them. "Be it unto you," our
Lord was constantly saying, " according to
your faith." He might have instituted some
other principle for His purpose than faith,
but it did not seem good to Him to do so.
And thus it is, that from beginning to end
of the Christian life, and from centre to cir-
cumference, it is faith first, faith last, faith

always, faith everywhere. And nowhere more
than just here and in the practice of the
presence of God. Practise faith then upon
the presence of God, and that will give God
a nearness to you and a reality to you and
a power over you that nothing else can do.
Believe that He is ever with you, as He is.
Believe that He is about your path and about
your bed, as He is. And because you say
every morning, "When I awake I am with
Thee," as you are; and seven, and ten, and a
hundred times every day fall back upon His
Omnipresence with you, He will not fail you.
Keep on believing and your joy will soon be
full—" For His presence is salvation."

(2) It is a very noble and ennobling practice
that some men have of connecting God's
presence with all His work in nature and in
providence as well as in grace. It is a very
comely and a very fruitful habit of mind—
or, I should rather say, a habit of heart—to
see God's presence in all His processes and
operations going on all around us. We like
our work to be recognised and appreciated;
and in this, God has made us in His own
image. It was one of His bitterest charges
against Israel in Isaiah's day that they did

not " consider " Him.   On the other hand,
" He maketh His sun to shine," said our
Lord, as often as He looked up into the
summer sky.   And within—William Law
used to take his stand at his eastern window
till the sun began to climb up into the
morning sky, when he saluted his fellow-
servant in these and like terms : " Glorious
creature," he exclaimed, " of the glorious
Creator, come and let us serve and obey
Him for another day, according to His
ordinances."   And may be, " Let us never
see the sun rising, or shining, or setting,
that we do not say—' His sun.'   Nor the
moon, nor the stars, nor the sea, nor the
hills, nor the rivers, nor the four seasons."

I remember, as long ago as I can remember
anything, hearing Dr Burns Thomson, of the
Cowgate Mission, opening a flower-show in
his native town and mine.   And I see and
hear him at this moment as he waves his
hands over the stacks of flowers and says :
" My Father made them all."   And I never
to this day see a summer-garden, or a flower-
show, or a bouquet of beautiful flowers, that
I do not hear a voice in my heart saying
often, " My Father made them all."   Such

Divine wisdom is there in a word of faith and love fitly spoken in the open ear of a little child.

And then from nature and from God's presence in nature we will rise to practise His presence in His ever-loving and never-sleeping providence. In past history and in everyday history, in His daily newspapers as well as His inspired Word. And from that onwards and inwards to His daily and homely momentary providence of all kinds in our own life. " Practice produces perfection." And what a noble kind of perfection is here! No wonder that Brother Lawrence said that if he had a pulpit he would preach little else but the practice of the presence of God.

(3) The prophets and the psalmists of Israel made such splendid practice of this presence of the pure and absolute Godhead in their day, that, what they would have attained to, had they lived in our New Testament day, I cannot imagine. For how easy, and how pleasant, and how attractive, and how heart-winning it is to practise the presence of God in Christ. What a heart-entrancing, heart-satisfying

exercise is the presence of God in the fairest
of the sons of men! Do you do it, my
brethren? Do you practise the presence of
God in act? Begin to do it and you will
never leave off. I defy you to stop it once
you begin. And begin in this simple and
sincere way. Practise your presence back
beside His presence. Practise your presence
all up and down the four Gospels. Your
presence at His baptism, at His temptation
in the wilderness, at this sermon of His, and
that, also this miracle of His, and that, when
He is healing a leper, practising His part,
and possess yourself of the experience of that
unclean creature. When He is forgiving sins,
practise being the forgiven sinner. Practise
being Peter, Zacharias, and Mary Magdalen,
and the thief on the cross. Play their part
in the dramas. Appropriate their experiences in the Gospels. Practise, in that way,
every time you open the four Gospels; and
you will open them more than all other
books in the world, taken together, and
with good reason, till you will be one of the
greatest experts in the presence of God in it
now living on the face of the earth. And
then from that, go on to practise His presence

in it risen and glorified. Understanding all
the time that no small part of His glorifica-
tion stands in His power and His will to
be with you by His divine presence and by
His human sympathy, in ways and to results
past all your understanding, but only the
more sure to your experience. Practise His
risen presence in your personal life, in your
hours at home, in your secret heart. See
Him standing over you and inclining His
ear towards you in your most secret hour of
prayer. See Him sitting over against you,
when you sit down to do your work. Practise
a fast faith in Him in all your trials and in
all your crooked crosses. Enlist with yourself
to see His hand and no other hand, and to
salute but His, not only in the comforts and
the advantages and the enjoyments of life,
but almost more in the crosses and the con-
tradictions and the amputations and dis-
memberments of life.

Lay down this law to yourself—that
nothing comes to you of any kind without
His permission and even His ordination, and
you will soon be the man of the most serene
and most self-possessed heart in all the
world. So, practise His presence, both in

Scripture and still more in your own heart and life, till if He were to come into your house to-night and in the body, you would feel at once at home with Him and He with you.

Even to discourse in this way upon " the presence of God " is so repaying to me, that I can scarcely tear myself away from it. It is so good even to think and speak about it, let alone practising it. There is absolutely no end to the advantages and the rewards of it. Just to add this and then close ; when wearied to death with sin in our own hearts and when hunted to death with the occasions of sin and the provocations to sin in our own circumstances—what a refuge to us, what a rock to us, is this omnipresence of our God. *Deus ubique est : et totus ubique est :* was Augustine's constant refuge. Again—but let David describe it this time—" Thou shalt hide them in the secret of thy presence from the pride of men : thou shalt keep them secretly in a pavilion from the strife of tongues. Blessed be the Lord, for He hath showed me His marvellous kindness in a strong city."

And then, just one more morsel, by way

of acknowledgment to Brother Lawrence for his help this morning and his inspiration. " He had found such an advantage in living in this presence of God that it was natural for him to recommend it earnestly to others. But his example was a stronger inducement than any argument he could propose. His very countenance was edifying ; such a sweet and calm devotion appearing in it as could not but affect the beholder. And it was observed, that in the greatest hurry of business in his kitchen (for he was cook to the society), he still preserved his recollection and his heavenly-mindedness. He was never hasty, nor loitering, but did each thing in its season, with an even, uninterrupted composure and tranquillity of mind. ' The time of business,' said he, ' does not with me differ from the time of prayer, and in the noise and clatter of the kitchen, I possess God in as great tranquillity as if I were upon my knees before the Blessed Sacrament.' "

BIBLIOGRAPHY

The Bible.

Dionysius the Areopagite, Part II, 'The Heavenly Hierarchy'.

Dante, especially the third part of the *Divina Commedia*.

Goethe's *Faust*.

The Works of Swedenborg.

The Works of Blake.

Chambers's Encyclopedia. Article on 'Angels'.

Jewish Encyclopedia, Volume I. Article on 'Angelology' gives the place of Angels in the Jewish system.

Hastings' Encyclopædia of Religion and Ethics. Article on 'Angels'.

Life of St Columba, by Adamnan.

The Dream of Gerontius, by Cardinal Newman.

Apocalyptic Problems, by Very Rev. H. Erskine Hill.

Morgenrothe, by John Pulsford.

Saint Joan, by Bernard Shaw.

The Candle of Vision, by George Russell (Æ.).

Francis Thompson's Works.

Dante. Illustrations by Phœbe Anna Traquair, Notes by John Sutherland Black. Privately printed by T. and A. Constable.[1]

[1] It was one of the highest privileges of my life to help Walter B. Blaikie in the editing of this volume.

APPENDIX

APPENDIX

Dante

THIS Appendix on Dante is given to meet the need of those who have not studied the great Italian poet, so as to give them some indication of the large part which the hierarchies of angels play in the third division of the *Commedia*. It consists of quotations from C. E. Wheeler's Introductions to the Cantos of the *Paradiso*.

They pass through the sphere of fire and hear the harmonies of heaven.

Canto i.

Beatrice then explains that Dante has gone wrong and accepted a scientifically inadequate explanation, because he has not understood that all heavenly phenomena are direct utterances of God and of His angels. The undivided power of God, differentiated through the various heavenly bodies and agencies, shines in the diverse quality and brightness of the fixed stars, of the planets and of the parts of the moon, as the vital principle manifests itself diversely in the several members of the body, and as joy beams through the pupil of the eye.

Canto ii.

Beatrice, rejoicing in Dante's progress, explains the supreme gift of Free Will, shared by angels and men and by no other creature.

Canto v.

The spirit (Justinian) so glows with joy that his outward form is lost in light.

Canto v.

All angels, heavens and blessed spirits, from the Seraphim nearest God outwards, are twined in one concerted cosmic dance; this dance the spirits in Venus leave to minister to Dante, singing Hosanna as they come; and one of them declares their kinship of movement and of love with the celestial beings to whom he had once addressed his love hymn.

Canto viii.

The spirit whirls and glows, rapt into such immediate and intense communion with God as to see His very essence, and yet declares that neither he nor the highest of the Seraphim sees the answer to this question, which lies unfathomably deep in the being of God. Let Dante warn the world, with its smoke-dimmed faculties, not to presume henceforth to attempt a problem which even in heaven is insoluble. Appalled by this reply, Dante now bashfully requests to know who it is that has thus checked his presumptuous enquiry, and he learns that it is Peter Damiani, who called himself Peter the Sinner, and who had dwelt in the now degenerate convent of Fonte Avellana, and in that of S. Maria in Pomposa. In connection with his reception, shortly before his death, of the Cardinal's hat, he denounces the pomp and obesity of the Church dignitaries, whereupon there comes whirling down a throng of flames that group themselves round him and raise a cry which so stuns Dante that he understands not what it says.

Canto xxi.

Contemplation alone can lead to this timeless and spaceless life, whence the Jacob's ladder, that Dante's human eye cannot follow to its summit, is planted upon the star of abstinence and contemplation, and reaches to the heaven which Jacob saw it touch. But now none mounts this ladder, for all the monastic orders are degenerate.

Canto xxii.

Yet God has ere now wrought greater wonders than the renewal of their spirit would be. Therefore there is yet hope.

Canto xxii.

Thereon Dante at once perceives that the nine circles represent the Intelligences of angelic orders connected with the nine revolving heavens, but cannot see why the outmost, swiftest, widest sweeping and most divine heaven should cor-

respond with the inmost and smallest angelic
circle. Beatrice explains that the divine substance
of the heavens being uniform, that heaven which
is materially greatest has in it the most of excellence ; but it is the excellence, not the size, that
is essential. In like manner swiftness and brightness are the measure of the excellence of the
angelic circles, and therefore the inmost of them
which is swiftest and brightest represents those
intelligences that love and know most ; and the
spiritual correspondence is complete between the
two diverse spacial presentations. Thus the re-
lativity of space-conceptions is suggested. God
may be conceived as the spaceless centre of the
universe just as well as the all-embracer. Dante,
now enlightened, sees the circles shoot out count-
less sparks that follow them in their whirling,
and hears them all sing Hosanna ; while Beatrice
further explains how the swift joy of the angels
is proportioned to their sight, their sight to their
merit, won by grace and by exercise of will ;
whereas love is not the foundation but the in-
evitable consequence of knowledge. She has ex-
plained the three hierarchies and nine orders of
the angels, as Dionysius (enlightened by his own
intense passion of contemplation, and instructed
by Paul who had been rapt to heaven) had set
them forth.

Canto xxviii.

Beatrice tells him that they have now issued
forth from the heaven that compasses all space
into the heaven of light, love, joy, which is not a

thing of space, and where he shall behold the angels, and shall see the elect in the forms they will wear after the resurrection.

Canto xxx.

The redeemed are seen, rank above rank, as the petals of the divine rose ; and the angels flying between them and God minister peace and ardour to them, for passion is here peaceful and peace passionate.

Canto xxxi.